RADICAL LIBERTARIANISM

A Right Wing Alternative

RADICAL LIBERTARIANISM

A New Political Alternative

JEROME TUCCILLE

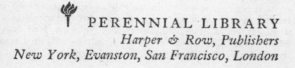

PERENNIAL LIBRARY
Harper & Row, Publishers
New York, Evanston, San Francisco, London

A hardcover edition of this book was published originally by The Bobbs-Merrill Company, Inc.

To my wife, Marie, who was there when it counted.

With special thanks to KARL HESS, DR. MURRAY N. ROTHBARD, LEONARD LIGGIO, and WALTER BLOCK, whose dedication to justice has shown me that libertarian principles could be more than just an intellectual pastime.

CONTENTS

INTRODUCTION TO THE PERENNIAL EDITION

"A New Political Alternative"

When *Radical Libertarianism* first appeared in hardcover in the summer of 1970, it carried the subtitle: *A Right Wing Alternative*. My reasons for changing this subtitle for the paperback edition merit some explanation here. The old terminology of Left and Right is becoming more obsolete as our major political parties resemble each other more every day. The difference from "liberal" Left and "conservative" Right is no longer a proper distinction. Establishment politics has become a matter of two broad factions fighting each other for control of a highly centralized political structure. There are forces at work in our society, some using the rhetoric of individualism and free-marketism and others the language of collectivism and neighborhood socialism, which are acting to decentralize political power and break it down into small units —eventually to the level of the individual.

So who is Left and who is Right? Perhaps we should throw out such labels altogether. But as long as people continue to speak in terms of Left Wing and Right Wing, collectivism and individualism, new definitions are in order to help us understand exactly what we mean when we use language that is becoming as outdated as yesterday's newspaper.

The psychology of Left and Right manifests itself on various levels and it is quickly becoming the only way to identify an individual in terms of Left Wing and Right Wing terminology. We have seen the collapse of old-time ideologies over the past few years, and the distinction between left-of-center welfare statists and right-of-center free enterprisers is no longer valid.

In the political lexicon of today anyone with a strong commitment to the preservation of our present system may be labeled a "conservative," and this includes crusty old New Dealers like Jacob Javits, Lyndon Johnson and Hubert Humphrey who were considered radical innovators back in the 1930s. These establishmentarians who still get by under the name of "liberalism" are slightly less conservative than the Buckleys and Nixons in the sense that they recognize the need for continuing reforms, and with few exceptions they are not so bloodthirsty in their desire to repress radical attacks on the status quo. But these liberals, or the New Conservatives who are so adroit at using reactionist conservatives as the police arm of the corporate-liberal state, are dedicated centralists to the core of their convictions.

While recognizing the need for continuing reforms, the liberals or New Conservatives are determined at the same time that these reforms will be implemented from the top by their own people, by their own special crowd of think-tank intellectuals and professional experts. They are also shrewd enough to understand that the demand for decentralized authority in the United States is one to be heeded if we are to avoid large-scale civil war. This they are out to avoid at all costs since it would mean the end of their rule, the end of their power, the final collapse of the heavily centralized social democracy through which they hoped to bring the egalitarian millennium to the masses. Accordingly, the New Conservatives have been quick to pick up the language of decentralization, the rhetoric of Power-to-the-People, Power-to-the-Neighborhoods, while attempting to carry on their social reforms by means of a central planning authority. In this they are different from the reactionist conservatives; those who wear the mantle of conservatism rarely concern themselves with co-optation, preferring instead to bludgeon the opposition out of existence in the name of all that's good and holy.*

In view of the New Conservatives' reliance on the power of co-optation, they could have been nothing but mortified by the provisions for a new constitution proposed by the Center for the Study of Democratic Institutions.‡ This is primarily the brain-child of Rexford Guy Tugwell, an old-style New Dealer, who had apparently been so isolated in an ivory tower atmosphere during the drafting of this document that he hadn't deigned to read a news-

---

* An exception is Richard Nixon who seems to have learned his lessons in co-optation well from the liberals.
‡ New York Times, September 8, 1970.

paper or watch a newscast for six years. The special arrogance of the proposed constitution reflects the thinking of a man who not only does not know what has been going on in the streets of our cities the last few years, but doesn't even care that the current agitation is for *less,* not more power in the hands of the federal government. There has been remarkably little comment about this document from liberals more attuned to the temper of our times; they see it as a potential timebomb which will kick up a storm on both the radical Left and reactionist Right and they have wisely decided to play hands-off for the time being.

Briefly, the proposed constitution calls for the re-division of the United States into no more than twenty republics with severely limited powers; a nine-year term for the President with a provision that he or she could be removed after three years if the people so decided—a provision that would prove to be about as effective as impeachment procedures are today; two Vice Presidents with shared authority; and a Senate elected for *life*. Other changes call for a revamping of the House of Representatives, the judicial system and a new bill of rights with individual freedoms more narrowly defined than in the original.

This is hardly a "liberal" proposal in the strict sense of the word. At one time *liberal* was synonymous with freedom: without restraint, open, flexible, the polar opposite of authoritarian. Now we see that this term in its present politial context is virtually stripped of its original meaning; certainly it is difficult to visualize a more *conservative* and authoritarian document than the one described above, unless one favors outright dictatorship. If American liberalism has come to this, a new term is drastically in order for we are destroying language completely and deceiving ourselves with a strange brand of Orwellian doublethink. The term *New Conservative* describes the old liberals as well as any other, with the term *reactionist conservative* more accurately defining the more traditionalist concept of repressive Right Wing opposition to attacks against the status quo.

If welfare statism has taken on a Right Wing hue in the last few years, with reactionist and New Conservatives bound together in a common crusade to preserve the present system, then a new definition of exactly what the Left is also is in order. Radical and even moderate decentralists are politically Left in the sense that they are in opposition to centralized Right Wing power. In the contemporary scheme of things the regime in Moscow is as Right Wing as the admittedly rightist regimes of Greece and Spain; Moscow communists were even labeled hard-line Right Wingers by the Czechoslovakian rebels who sought to decentralize their own society in August of 1968. In the context of that struggle the decentralizers, the would-be "liberalizers" of Czechoslovakian society were radicals of the extreme Left in opposition to unyielding centralist authority.

It makes little difference in a practical sense whether the centralized political structure carries a

Left Wing label, communism, or goes under the Right Wing name of fascism. The tendency toward centralized authority is as debilitating for the individual in any case, and while corporate liberalism in the United States, England, Sweden, etc., is not yet as demoralizing as undisguised dictatorship, it is distinctly "Right Wing" in that it acts to draw power away from the people and into the maw of a depersonalized Monolith.

If, then, political decentralization has come to be identified with the Left, not only in America but on a world scale, it becomes apparent that free marketism or laissez faire, which is nothing more or less than *decentralization down to the level of the individual*, has once again resumed its heritage as a *phenomenon of the Left*. We can see that the talk of a Left-Right alliance has already become a reality in political definition when it is taken to mean an alliance between radical decentralists and free market libertarians. They are forced together *by definition* in a society which is radically polarized and which sees itself in terms of black and white, in terms of opposites. With the polarization that has occurred in American society there is very little room left for fence-straddling. There are few "moderates" left in the sense the word had back in the early 1960s. People are almost forced to choose one side or the other in a barricade situation, and the political barricades in the United States are as sharply evident now as they have been in a long time.

As the new decade unfolds we find ourselves in a situation where *neighborhood socialists* and an-

archists of the *free market school* are actually occupying the same side, the Left, of a widening
political gap in the United States. How can it be
that *socialists* and *radical capitalists* find themselves
on the same ground in any political division? The
paradox seems unnerving if we think of it in terms
of the old labels. In the present American situation
the ideals of neighborhood socialism and laissez-
faire capitalism are actually closer in practice than
they appear to be in rhetoric. Both are idealistic
in that they tend toward divergent utopian goals,
one toward a peaceful communal society, the other
toward a peaceful world of free individual traders.
In practice, however, neither dream can be fully
realized outside the fantasy world of incorrigible
utopians. The best that either school, the anarcho-
socialists and the free market anarchists, can hope
for within the next thirty years is some sort of compromise accommodation with each other, some form
of decentralized neighborhood structure in which
some communities, most likely the more affluent,
will take on a more individualistic tone and others,
primarily poorer neighborhoods, will be more com-
munity-oriented.

Perhaps we need a new language to define all this,
some terminology other than "socialism" or "capitalism"; until someone comes up with something
better, *anarchism* or *libertarianism* will have to serve
the purpose.

The ingredient which renders the situation all
the more difficult to understand is the fact that the
forces for centralization—the Right Wing as we

have defined it in this chapter—have also retained the old terminology of "socialism" versus "capitalism." The New Conservatives, the social democrats or old-line liberals, still think of themselves as basically socialistic in their social and economic attitudes, while the reactionist conservatives invariably refer to themselves as free enterprisers. Actually neither self-image is correct. The status quo they have erected and which they propose to defend in common is neither socialism nor capitalism and it is therefore important that a new word be found to define the present system.

Since it is a centralized political structure, heavily planned and managed from the top, the mixed economy condition that exists in most of the large western democratic republics has been labeled both *state socialism* and *state capitalism* by various political analysts—the main distinction being that in the former case there is a tendency toward some nationalization of industry, and in the latter toward management rather than nationalization. Using this somewhat shaky analysis as our criterion, the condition supported by both New and reactionist conservatives in the United States is a variation of state capitalism, with some talk lately of incorporating into it some state socialist measures (nationalization of the railroads and utilities has been suggested in some circles).

Consequently, some quasi-libertarian intellectuals of both socialistic and capitalistic schools who are reluctant to divorce themselves completely from the "establishment" have identified more closely with either the liberals (New Conservatives) or conservatives (reactionist conservatives) almost exclusively on grounds of rhetoric. Milton Friedman, calling himself a philosophical free market anarchist, attaches himself to a reactionist political administration because it continues to talk the language of free enterprise; Norman Mailer, who ran for Mayor of New York City on a radical decentralist platform, still primarily identifies with liberals since they have retained a Left Wing rhetoric. And so the division runs all the way down the line, with many anarcho-capitalists feeling more comfortable in the company of Ronald Reagan than they do with Eugene McCarthy, and anarcho-socialists swinging better with Gene than with Barry Goldwater.

Here we enter the realm of psychological opposites. The long-term test of whether an individual will identify with the Left or with the Right is one of personal psychology. The psychology of Left and Right manifests itself on several levels.

In the broadest sense, Left-Wing psychology operates in terms of concretes. Left Wingers are more apt to see the world in its specific reality; they experience the sights and sounds and smells of poverty; the empathize with the actual victims of injustice and therefore have a more naturalistic understanding of what injustice means. Left Wingers are probably more feeling-oriented in the sense that they are more willing to break a philosophical principle to rectify an unjust situation. Even if they *do not believe* in robbing the rich to feed the poor they may be willing to do so if they see someone going hungry. They are also philosophical in the sense that they intellectualize their own attitudes, but they are usually not so bound by philosophical absolutes that they will not break one for the sake of relieving someone else's misery.

The Right Wing mentality, on the other hand, deals almost exclusively with abstractions. The Right Wing anarchist is also against injustice and on the side of liberty, but he is more likely to become more incensed because his *theories* are not being put into operation than he is because somebody's baby was bitten by a rat. He knows that there is discrimination in the world, that some people are denied decent housing and adequate employment, but he is more annoyed at the "irrationality" of this condition than he is by its real-life effect on human beings. Not only is the psychological Right Winger usually unconcerned about the specifics of injustice, he will denounce all sympathy for the misery of others as immoral altruism.

Both psychological Left Wingers and psychological Rightists can be violently anti-state, but their different psychological attitudes will flavor the nature of their anti-statist motivation. The Left Wingers will fight the authorities, even to the point of sacrificing their own lives, as long as there is one little pocket of injustice remaining in the world; the efforts of the Right Wing anarchist will be directed toward securing his own personal freedom and putting his theories into practice if only on a limited scale. The psychology of the Left is primarily *ltruistic* and *world-oriented;* that of the Right *sel-fish* and *ego-oriented.* From this we can see that the psychology of Left and Right can co-exist within the framework of a *Left Wing political* perspective (in the case of anti-establishment radicals), and also within the framework of a *Right Wing political* perspective (in the case of pro-establishment liberals and conservatives).

The great danger inherent in this condition is that the psychological Right Winger may abandon his Left Wing political position and align with the Right *whenever the going gets too rough.* His doctrinaire selfishness renders his mania for self-preservation paramount over all other considerations, and he may temporarily renew his alliance with his Right Wing political counterpart in a crisis situation. The psychological Left Winger runs the risk of being so self*less* and other-oriented that he will be driven to Left Wing adventurism (à la the Weathermen) if his goals are not achieved tomorrow. In other words, the radical movement can be derailed on both counts—by the psychological Rightist who will compromise his political principles to save his own neck; by the psychological Leftist who will adopt suicidal tactics in the cause of his service to humanity.

With these considerations out of the way, perhaps we can now sit down and analyze some of the problems we are currently facing in our society, and come up with some concrete alternatives.

RADICAL LIBERTARIANISM

A Right Wing Alternative

LIBERTARIANS VS. CONSERVATIVES:

Confrontation on the Right

"Are Libertarians and Conservatives natural allies, or are they, in fact, polar opposites?" economist/ writer Murray Rothbard asks in advertisements for his libertarian journal, *Left and Right*. Conservatives claim to be champions of individual freedom, advocates of limited government organized strictly for the purpose of defending the individual from domestic violence and the country at large from international aggression, devoted passionately to the creation of a laissez-faire society with equal liberties for each and every individual. At least, such is the claim in articles appearing in *Human Events, National Review, Rally, Modern Age, The Intercollegiate Review, Triumph,* and other conservative publications throughout the country. But gradually, more and more vociferously and with increasing frequency, this claim is coming under strong attack, not from the liberal opposition that has traditionally questioned the libertarian posture of the right, but from a growing new alliance of disaffected "conservative" intellectuals.

One of the most eloquent challenges to the modern conservative mentality was made by Karl Hess, former speechwriter for Senator Barry Goldwater, who announced his support for many of the New Left objectives in a well-publicized interview. In his article "The Death of Politics," which appeared in the March 1969 issue of *Playboy*, Hess began by summing up the libertarian position.

Libertarianism is the view that each man is the absolute owner of his life, to use and dispose of it as he sees fit; that all man's social actions should be voluntary; and that respect for every other man's similar and equal ownership of life and, by extension, the property and fruits of that life, is the ethical basis of a humane and open society. In this view, the only function of law or government is to provide the sort of self-defense against violence that an individual, if he were powerful enough, would provide for himself. "The socioeconomic form" of this radical revolutionary position "is laissez-faire capitalism."

After stating his initial premise, Hess then proceeds to excoriate the modern conservative on several accounts.

Capitalism is rejected by the modern right—which preaches enterprise but practices protectionism. The libertarian faith in the mind of man is rejected by reli-

gionists who have faith only in the sins of man. . . .
The libertarian insistence that each man is a sovereign
land of liberty, with his primary allegiance to himself,
is rejected by patriots who sing of freedom but also
shout of banners and boundaries.

Again, on the subject of capitalism:

Big business in America today and for some years
past has been openly at war with competition and,
thus, at war with laissez-faire capitalism. Big business
supports a form of state capitalism in which government and big business act as partners. . . . Men who
call themselves conservatives, but who operate in the
larger industries, spend considerable time, and not a
small amount of money, fighting government subsidies
to labor unions. . . . They do not fight *direct* subsidies
to industries—such as transportation, farming or uni-
versities. . . . It is safe to say that the major powers of
government to regulate industry were derived not only
from the support of businessmen but actually at the insistence of businessmen . . . [Lenny Bruce] was . . . a
particularly favorite target of conservatives. He was
also an explicit and, I think, incisive defender of capitalism. In commenting that communism is a drag ["like
one big phone company"], Bruce specifically opted for
capitalism ("it gives you a choice, baby, and that's
what it's about"). There is no traditional conservative
who is fit to even walk on the same level with Lenny
Bruce in his fierce devotion to individualism.

Hess is equally explicit on the issue of Law-and-
Order:

[Getting tough] does not mean just getting tough
on rioters. It means . . . clipping long hair, rousting

people from parks for carrying concealed guitars, stopping and questioning anyone who doesn't look like a member of the Jaycees, drafting all the ne'er-do-wells to straighten them up, ridding our theaters and bookstores of "filth" and always and above all putting "those" people in their place.

A point which many people in the United States have not fully understood is the fact that Christianity, the traditional religion of conservatives, is closely tied in with this whole concept of Law-and-Order.

It was conservatives . . . who ceded to the state the power to produce not simply order in the community but a *certain kind of order*. [Conservatives] seem to think that the state is an institution divinely ordained to make man moral—in a "Judeo-Christian" sense of course.

On this point, Hess's challenge is supported by Murray Rothbard, libertarian economist and editor of *Left and Right*. According to Rothbard, a new generation of conservatives seems to feel that the real issue is *not* one of state vs. individual liberty or government intervention vs. the free market. "The real problem" to them "is the preservation of tradition, order, Christianity and good manners against the modern sins of reason, license, atheism and boorishness."

This fissure on the right, which is now dividing the pro-capitalist community between libertarians and conservatives, rationalists and mystics, atheists (or agnostics) and religionists, radical individualists and Christian collectivists, is not new with Hess and Rothbard. The seeds of this latest eruption were planted in 1958 with the publication of Ayn Rand's long, philosophical novel, *Atlas Shrugged*. Although the book leaves much to be desired as a work of fiction, it is extremely important as a fully realized and completely developed philosophical statement. *Atlas Shrugged* was an uncompromising, unequivvocating defense of individualism, unregulated capitalism, egoism, rational self-interest, reason, objective reality, and absolute values. At the same time, Objectivism (the name Miss Rand gave to her philosophy) attacked the traditional sacred cows of the modern right: Christianity and its ethical component altruism, sacrifice, faith, original sin, their belief in the supernatural, the Calvinistic view that man is inherently evil rather than fundamentally rational and creative. Predictably enough, the book was taken apart with religious zeal and precision in the pages of William F. Buckley's *National Review*. Miss Rand had struck a severe blow at the precise spot where conservatives are most vulnerable: their basic premises. According to Ayn Rand, the traditionalist conservatives had erected a house of cards in attempting to defend capitalism in terms of Christian ethics. She made the point that capitalism is a fundamentally egoistic concept and consequently demands an ethic based on self-interest rather than altruism, reason instead of faith, man instead of God, objective reality rather than supernaturalism. Buckley was quick to recognize Miss Rand as an enemy rather than a pro-capitalist ally. In effect, she was telling him and conservatives at large that they were living a contradiction—that their moral principles were totally incompatible with their political and economic convictions.

This philosophical rift can be traced back a good deal further than the 1950s. Libertarianism is basically Aristotelian (reason, objectivity, individual self-sufficiency) while conservatism is just as fundamentally Platonic (privileged elitism, mysticism, collective order). More recently, the basic elements of Objectivism can be seen in the writings of nineteenth-century anarchists Benjamin Tucker, Lysander Spooner, Stephen P. Andrews, and Max Stirner, while the conservative tradition owes its heritage to a grab bag mixture of classical liberals, such as Bentham, Locke, Hume, and Rousseau, and royalists such as Edmund Burke.

Ironically, many philosophical disciples of Ayn Rand have lately grown disenchanted with what they interpret as a "conservative Law-and-Order" position Miss Rand has taken on such issues as the military draft, payment of taxes, property rights. The woman who once said that an individual had the absolute right to defend himself against violence in any form, whether it be perpetrated by another individual, a gang, or government itself, put herself in the compromising position of stating publicly on Johnny Carson's *Tonight* program that no one had the right to break a law unless he was trying to make a test case out of it. Thus a woman who created one hero (Howard Roark) who dynamited a public housing project, and another (Ragnar) who attacked foreign-aid freighters on the open seas because of their unyielding individualistic views, now comes out on the side of Law-and-Order against a young man who refuses to be drafted into a jungle war halfway around the earth. Consequently many Objectivists, while still adhering to the basic formulations of her philosophy, have now taken a more independent course.

Before Ayn Rand fictionalized her libertarian doctrine in the form of *Atlas Shrugged*, individual freedom had its champions on the Old Right in many first-rate intellectuals whose names, ironically, have been largely lost to the current generation of liberty-seekers. In fact, the laissez-faire position of the Old Right has been distorted out of recognition by the crop of liberal intellectuals who succeeded it in the middle and late '50s. It might be worthwhile to point out that such positions as open resistance to the military draft, conservation of our natural resources, non-involvement in the affairs of other nations, isolationism in military matters, decentralization and community control, and a host of issues which are of paramount importance to the New Left today were identified with right-wing Republicanism as recently as the early 1950s. It was only during the anti-Communist witch-hunting era in the middle 1950s, institutionalized by an *establishment liberal*, Senator Joe McCarthy, that the right-wing abandoned its championship of individual liberty and embarked upon its sorry course of fanatical anti-

communism. With the advent of crusading conservative religionists such as Russell Kirk and William F. Buckley, the freedom of the individual was
to be subordinate to the traditions of the state in
the lexicon of the Right. While giving lip-service
resistance to the ever-expanding federal bureaucracy which conservatives had been railing against,
at least theoretically, since the inauguration of the
welfare state, the conservatives had in fact helped
the liberals launch the warfare state with their un-
holy obsession to exterminate atheistic Communists
at any and all costs. This is where the New Right
stands today, and it is with a sense of loss, nostalgia,
and some degree of sadness that one re-reads the
writings of Old Right libertarians Frank Chodorov,
Garet Garrett, Albert Jay Nock, H. L. Mencken,
Frederick C. Smith, Robert Taft, Dean Russell, and
so many other brilliant champions of the individual
man.

Consider, for instance, the following samples of
intellectual Old Right opinion and ask yourself if
such ideas are more likely to be found today in the
pages of the conservative *National Review* or a
New Left journal such as *Ramparts*.

Even if it were desirable, America is not strong
enough to police the world by military force. If that
attempt is made, the blessings of liberty will be replaced
by coercion and tyranny at home. . . . We cannot
practice might and force abroad and retain freedom at
home. We cannot talk world cooperation and practice
power politics.

This was Representative Howard Buffett attacking Harry S. Truman's foreign policy just before the Korean war.

Or read Dean Russell, who wrote on the military draft and foreign wars in May of 1955:

Those who advocate the "temporary loss" of our freedom in order to preserve it permanently are advocating only one thing: the abolition of liberty. . . . These sincere but highly emotional people are clear and present threats to freedom. . . . As long as we keep troops in countries on Russia's borders, the Russians can be expected to act somewhat as we would act if Russia were to station troops in Guatemala or Mexico. . . . I can see no more logic in fighting Russia over Korea or Outer Mongolia, than in fighting England over Cypress, or France over Morocco. . . . Facts of imperialism . . . are not sufficient reasons to justify . . . turning ourselves into a permanent garrison state. . . .

Then there is the right-fing "extremist" Frank Chodorov, writing on the nature of the state in his monthly journal, *Analysis:*

. . . the state is an anti-social organization, originating in conquest and concerned only with confiscating production. . . .

The state is that group of people, who having got hold of the machinery of compulsion, legally or otherwise, use it to better their circumstances . . . the state consists not only of politicians, but also those who make use of the politicians for their own ends . . . pressure group, lobbyists and all who would wangle special privileges out of the politicians. . . .

In 1951, Dr. F. A. Harper published an essay, "In Search of Peace," with a right-wing imprint (Foundation for Economic Education). In it he spoke of pacifism:

If pacifism means embracing the objective of peace, I am willing to accept the charge. If it means opposing all aggression against others, I am willing to accept the charge also. It is now urgent in the interest of liberty that many persons become "peacemongers". . . . False ideas can be attacked only with counter-ideas, facts and logic . . . the ideas of Karl Marx [cannot] be destroyed today by murdering innocent victims of the form of slavery be advocated. . . .

Then there is perhaps one of the greatest American muckrakers of all time, H. L. Mencken, writing in his book, *A Mencken Crestomathy* (Knopf, 1949):

. . . When a private citizen is robbed, a worthy man is deprived of the fruits of his industry and thrift; when the government is robbed, the worst that happens is that certain rogues and loafers have less money to play with than they had before. . . . Is it a fact of no significance that robbing the government is everywhere regarded as a crime of less magnitude than robbing an individual, or even a corporation? . . . [Government] is apprehended, not as a committee of citizens chosen to carry on the communal business of the whole population, but as a separate and autonomous corporation, mainly devoted to exploiting the population for the benefit of its own members. . . .

Compare this with the right-wing writings of today, with the rhetoric of the New Right journal,

National Review, in which "peacemonger" Senator William Fulbright is denounced as a traitor and all those opposed to the deployment of an ABM system are branded cowards.

Clearly the wheel has come full cycle: the libertarian Right has rediscovered the Old Right policies of the late '40s and early '50s, and the conservatives now spout the anti-Communist paranoia handed on to them by the New Dealers of twenty years ago.

The organization that is most visibly shaken by this libertarian/conservative rift on the right is the campus-affiliated Young Americans for Freedom. Traditionally conservative in conception, YAF is now divided by frequent confrontations between traditionalist and libertarian members. An assistant chairman of the Eastern Pennsylvania Council of YAF has loudly announced a policy of "consistent and sometimes radical libertarianism." He is joined in this position by most of the upper echelon leaders of his division and of many other divisions across the country, some of whom are now considering more militant tactics, akin to those of the New Left, to protest the military draft, increasing taxation, sex and abortion laws, censorship regulations, licensing of television and radio stations, destruction of private property by various levels of government, school centralization, and a whole list of grievances against ever-increasing state authority. On many of these issues their aims, if not their reasoning, are identical with those of the New Left, and it is possible that some sort of alliance may eventually be formed to achieve common goals. So far, no YAF libertarians have gone as far as Karl Hess who has come out in support of SDS. The thinking is that SDS activism is indiscriminate, displaying equal contempt for offensive institutions and innocent individuals alike, that SDS leadership is without coherent intellectual and philosophical form, even irrational in nature, and therefore represents a negative rather than a positive force for libertarian progress. However, much of the *membership* of SDS is motivated by libertarian thinking and an attempt is being made to attract genuine libertarian radicals into a left/right coalition.

Because of the growing libertarian agitation within YAF, many traditionalist conservatives have already begun to attack the organization as being "infiltrated by left-wing radicals." If YAF does take a more militant posture regarding issues, on or off campus, it will put them in direct opposition to traditionalist conservative leaders William F. Buckley, Jr., Frank S. Meyer, James Burnham, Russell Kirk, Henry Paolucci, John Chamberlain, M. Stanton Evans, and others who have come out in favor of complete suppression of student radicalism and a return to Christian obedience in society at large.

The presidential election campaign of 1968 was another issue which further divided libertarians and conservatives. Libertarians recognized George C. Wallace's brand of "populist conservatism" as nothing more than a vulgar form of semi-literate fascism.

For the most part, conservatives supported Richard Nixon over Wallace only because he happened to be the better choice of the two. If the election were narrowed to a choice between Hubert Humphrey and George C. Wallace, there is no question that Wallace would have gotten a sizable portion of the conservative vote while libertarians would have stayed home rather than vote for either candidate.

In subsequent chapters we will discuss the issues of Black Power, decentralization, anarchist alternatives to hardline "liberal" and "conservative" positions, the question of capitalism vs. socialism as an issue dividing left-wing and right-wing libertarians and what can be done to resolve it, a common meeting ground for libertarians and the New Left, and acceptable tactics in the fight to achieve a free and open society.

In closing this chapter it should be stated that at the present time it appears certain that the rift which has developed between libertarians and conservatives is too fundamental to be healed. It is not a simple falling-out because of differences of opinion over specific issues. It is a deeply-rooted philosophical division over basic premises that have their origins as far back in history as Aristotle and Plato. It is a philosophical division that has manifested itself at various times throughout the course of European history and is only now coming to the surface in the United States. It is too early to say exactly what effect this division will have on the shape of American politics in the years to come, but it is certain to have a profound influence on the intellectual and cultural climate of the nation that will last far into the future.

TWO

BLACK POWER AND THE CONSERVATIVE DILEMMA

Twenty years ago I was an extreme right-wing Republican, young and lone "Neanderthal" (as the liberals used to call us) who believed, as one friend pungently put it, that "Senator Taft had sold out to the socialists." Today I am most likely to be called an extreme leftist, since I favor immediate withdrawal from Vietnam, denounce U. S. imperialism, advocate Black Power. . . . And yet my basic political views have not changed by a single iota in these two decades.

It is obvious that something is very wrong with the old labels, with the categories of "left" and "right," and with the ways in which we customarily apply these categories to American political life . . . if I can move from "extreme right" to "extreme left" merely by standing in one place. . . .

So writes Murray Rothbard in his article "Confessions" which appeared in *Ramparts*, June 15, 1968.

If there is one issue over which libertarians and conservatives take uniformly opposite positions it is the subject of Black Power. Most libertarians have been quick to realize that the current agitation in the black community for local control of their own affairs and individualistic rather than social welfare programs to advance their own economic status, is totally compatible with libertarian principles. On the other hand, traditionalist conservatives are afraid of anything that has a "black radical" label on it, regardless of whether or not it coincides with their own interests. *Human Events,* the weekly conservative newspaper published in Washington, D.C., has taken Roy Innis to task on a number of occasions because of the fact that he speaks of "Black Power" and is interested in "separatism" rather than artificial integration. The irrationality of this position is evident in the fact that *Human Events* has never been a champion of integration and has always been in favor of States' Rights, which has been nothing more than an effective way of guaranteeing racial separatism.

It is curious to consider that in the New York City mayoralty race of 1969 no candidate from either the "liberal" left (including Republican incumbent John V. Lindsay) or the "conservative" right came out in favor of complete community control in the public school dispute (excluding Norman Mailer, whose candidacy we will discuss in a later section). When one considers that conservatives have long been champions of the "neighborhood school" concept, particularly during the time when liberals were trying to bus children from the ghettos into all-white public school districts throughout Queens and other middle-income boroughs, their call for moderation along the road to decentralization comes as nothing less than hypocrisy. Neighborhood control was a valid concept when the white suburbs were threatened by "invasion" from the black ghettos, but when blacks relinquished the idea of forced integration and cried out for a stronger voice in hiring their own teachers and designing a meaningful curriculum for their children, the conservatives suddenly talked of compromise.

"I'm for some form of decentralization, but not the kind promoted by some people," said Vito P. Battista, founder of the United Taxpayers Party and conservative challenger to Mayor Lindsay in the Republican primary.

"With an elected board, the city would have a centralized system with a Board of Examiners, centralized assignment of teachers and principals and centralized maintenance of standards and quality." (The *New York Times*, April 20, 1969.)

Several years before, Mr. Battista was adamantly opposed to "centralized" decision-making on the busing issue.

"I want local participation, but not local control. . . . The local community should not tell the schools where they should or shouldn't go. The local community may not have the talent," he continued in the same interview.

However, according to Mr. Battista, local communities in his native borough of Queens evidently had the "talent" to tell busing advocates where to go and at the same time opt for control over their own neighborhood schools.

The case of Senator John J. Marchi, Conservative Party candidate for Mayor, is even more interesting. Mr. Marchi proposed a program calling for an "elected, seven-member central board which . . . could establish as many local districts as it wishes, provided each has at least 20,000 pupils." He then went on to say that the central board would retain the authority to hire and fire teachers and principals and establish a basic curriculum, while the local districts would be granted "certain limited powers": for instance, adding a few subjects to the curriculum to make it more relevant to the needs of the particular community, the ability to hire some technical and administrative personnel, a budget of $25,000 for the purpose of maintenance and repairs, and so on. In offering his program, Mr. Marchi put himself in the politically advantageous if unaccustomed position of receiving the support of the United Federation of Teachers (Albert Shanker's militant teachers' union) and Harry Van Arsdale's maintenance workers' union—big labor openly supporting the proposal of a Conservative Party candidate for Mayor.

Meanwhile the critical issue which was of paramount concern to ghetto residents—local control over the hiring of their own teachers and the establishment of a curriculum for their own children—

was abandoned by the traditional advocates of the "neighborhood school' concept.

Among the Democratic candidates (again, excluding Norman Mailer) the record was just as bad but consistent with the usual muddled "pragmatism" and relativistic problem-solving that characterizes so many of today's politicians. Herman Badillo, Puerto Rican Borough President of the Bronx, who styled himself as the most liberal of the Democrats, came out in favor of "some decentralization of authority" and for an "experiment with different approaches and methods." Among his profound observations was the comment that "Educational systems in all our major urban areas have failed in the ghetto neighborhoods." Similar statements were issued by the other Democratic candidates, from the liberals to "conservative" Mario Procaccino, who voiced his support for "parent involvement, parent participation" but his opposition to "the distortion of parent participation into one of complete community control." (The statements above were taken from the *New York Times*, April 20, 1969.) Most of the Democrats, while generally expressing the same sentiments as those expressed by Conservatives Battista and Marchi, did not even bother to be as explicit as the latter in their proposals for some sort of "centralized local control."

Without exception, their prime concern was enhancing their political positions by satisfying the militant, uncompromising posture of the UFT while at the same time appearing to be in sympathy with the demands emanating from the black ghettos.

The black community, once again, was betrayed by the machinations of power-seeking, vacillating politicians.

This quasi-paternal attitude toward blacks is not confined to the domestic scene. In his article "Hands Off Southern Africa," appearing in the March 1969, issue of *The Freeman*, a conservative monthly published in Irvington-on-Hudson, New York, journalist William Henry Chamberlain writes:

[Apartheid] is defended by most white South Africans and by some natives on the ground that a racially amalgamated society in South Africa is neither possible nor desirable, that the various races are happiest if given separate opportunities. . . . I visited [South Africa] in the spring of 1968 and came away with the feeling that the government was sincere in its ideal of racial separate development. . . .

Attributing sincerity to the South African government is nothing less than incredible when one considers the comments South African author, Alan Paton (*Cry the Beloved Country, Too Late the Phalarope*), made to me in a letter dated January 4, 1969:

You, however, do not know the latest development. In May, 1968, the government passed a law which forbade people of different racial groups to collaborate in any political organisation, and we [the Liberal Party] had only two courses open to us. One was to break up into separate parties each representing one racial group, or to disband. We chose the second course because we did not see how a party which came into being to fight against Apartheid could then consent to implement it in its own organisation.

This is not *voluntary* separatism that Mr. Chamberlain and Mr. Paton are talking about; it is *coercive* separatism—not freedom of association, but racial segregation enforced by the jackboot of the state. This is the policy that Mr. Chamberlain, "conservative" champion of individual freedom, dismisses as a sincere ideal of the government.

Libertarians recognize that the current demand in black communities for stronger local controls and the restructuring of public schools along the lines of smaller, privately-run institutions, is quite consistent with libertarian principles of individual freedom and decentralized government.

Across the country, a young, strong, militant libertarian voice is emerging from the black community. It is no surprise that it is sometimes loudest in New York City where the power of centralized government has already gone as far as it can possibly go without degenerating into undisguised dictatorship.

Sometimes this "black militancy" is also linked with "racial separatism," as in the case of Roy Innis, National Director of the Congress of Racial Equality (CORE), who seems to believe that black and white must go their own ways, at least until the blacks recover some measure of the self-esteem that was long ago confiscated by their white "masters." We have already seen that coercive separatism is even more destructive than coercive integration. But whenever separatism is taken to mean absolute freedom of association (voluntary integration for those who want it, voluntary separatism for others like Roy Innis), it should be supported by libertarians as a policy consistent with their own ideas. Voluntarism is the very foundation of liberty, and the right to separate voluntarily is equally as valid as the right to integrate voluntarily.

Libertarians should actively support black leaders such as Roy Innis, Dr. Thomas W. Matthew, founder of the National Economic Growth and Reconstruction Organization (NEGRO), Jim Brown, former football star and now an actor who has started his own program of financial assistance to black entrepreneurs, and other black leaders who are trying to solve the problems of the ghetto through voluntaristic rather than coercive means.

THREE

ANARCHY REDISCOVERED:

Popular Misconceptions

When arguments among delegates stalled the Pennsylvania constitutional convention for several months in its business of setting up a new government, life in the commonwealth passed uneventfully. Benjamin Franklin is said to have warned the delegates: "Gentlemen, you see that in the anarchy in which we live society manages much as before. Take care, if our disputes last too long, that the pepole do not come to think that they can very easily do without us."

. . . the word *anarchy* was used universally in the sense of disorder and confusion, and it is still adopted in that sense by the ignorant and by adversaries interested in distorting the truth. . . .

When Jefferson clothes the basic concept of Liberalism in the words, "That government is best which governs least," then Anarachists say with Thoreau: "That government is best which governs not at all."

(The above statements are from *Patterns of Anarchy*, edited by Krimerman and Perry, Doubleday, 1966.)

It is unfortunate that today, after so much has been written about anarchism by many diverse philosophers throughout the world, the mere mention of the word to most people conjures images of wild-eyed iconoclasts on a mission to destroy civilized society. It has become a popular device for modern politicians to promise to rid the country of "perpetrators of violence, revolutionaries and anarchists" in an effort to win the applause and the votes of their constituents. This is amusing, if not alarming, when one considers that the major "perpetrator of violence" in the world today is none other than government itself. (This will be discussed in greater detail in Chapter Six.) If politicians meant that they would rid the country of themselves, as members of an oppressive, authoritarian ruling elite, then one could understand the enthusiasm of the crowds that respond so jubilantly to such a statement. But it is difficult to understand how a conservative, who theoretically is supposed to be an enemy of paternalistic government and a friend of individual freedom, can cheer himself hoarse and promise to defend the status quo that he has been attacking so vehemently for the past thirty-five years.

It is also unfortunate that anarchism has become so closely identified with communism over the past fifty years that the two are now used almost synonymously. What is overlooked or ignored today is the wide, extensive body of literature on anarchist thought by some fine old American anarchists of the nineteenth century—men whose dedication to individualism and a truly *competitive* free-market economy would send the conservatives of today running to Washington for protective legislation. There was, of course, a powerful collectivist school of anarchist philosophy founded upon Marxist ideology; but, for the most part, their ideas of a socialized society were quite different from the dictatorial communism that exists throughout the world today.

In fact, anarchy, both of the individualistic and collectivist schools, stands in direct opposition to the statist trends that are reaching out and suffocating the spirit of mankind today.

Anarchism in its strictest sense means, literally, *without government.* But this does not mean *without order* or *without social structure* or even *without social organization.* What anarchy specifically calls for is complete individual freedom within a framework of *respect for, and willingness not to violate, the equally valid freedom of each and every individual in society.*

In this sense freedom is not to be taken as the same thing as individual license. My freedom does not give me the right to occupy someone else's property, to confiscate his earnings, or to attack him physically. Every individual has the right to his own life and to seek and provide for his own happiness on earth. He has the right to trade freely with others, to sell his labor for a mutually agreeable price, and keep his earnings and property without fear of having it stolen by anyone else, including government. To insure that the individual is secure in his person and property, a community of people with generally homogeneous interests would most likely elect to organize themselves for the purpose of protection and social cooperation. But anarchism *does* insist that any such organization be of a *voluntary nature*. Voluntary organization for mutually beneficial ends is not inconsistent with anarchist thought. This concept will be covered in detail in the next chapter.

Let us now turn to some of the nineteenth century advocates of anarchism and see what they had to say on the subject. First, the individualists.

Lysander Spooner based his anarchism on what he considered to be principles native to America. He believed that society should always be dependent on the consent of the people, and that the right of revolution is *inalienable* whenever any governmental organization begins to suppress fundamental individual freedom. In his book, *No Treason*, published in 1867, he writes:

. . . there is no difference, in principle—but only in degree—between political and chattel slavery. The former, no less than the latter, denies a man's ownership of himself and the products of his labor; and asserts that other men may own him, and dispose of him and his property, for their uses, and at their pleasure.

Again, in the same book:

Majorities, as such, afford no guarantees for justice, They are men of the same nature as minorities. They have the same passions for fame, power, and money, as minorities; and are liable and likely to be equally— perhaps more than equally, because more boldly— rapacious, tyrannical and unprincipled, if intrusted with power. . . . To say that majorities, as such, have a right to rule minorities, is equivalent to saying that minorities have, and ought to have, no rights, except such as majorities please to allow them.

. . . the whole [American] Revolution turned upon, asserted, and, in theory, established the right of each and every man, at his discretion, to release himself from the support of the government under which he had lived. And this principle was asserted . . . as a universal right of all men, at all times, and under all circumstances. . . .

On the subject of taxation he is equally explicit:

Either "taxation without consent is robbery," or it is not. If it is *not*, then any number of men . . . may assume absolute authority over all weaker than themselves; plunder them at will; and kill them if they resist. If . . . "taxation without consent *is* robbery," it necessarily follows that every man who has not consented to be taxed, has the same natural right to defend his property against a tax-gatherer, that he had to defend it against a highwayman.

Benjamin R. Tucker published his own journal, *Liberty*, from 1881 to 1908. His concept of social order was one based on "social contract" which he found compatible only with anarchism. In his volume of essays, *Instead of a Book*, published in New

York in 1893, he said, concerning the nature of government:

> The essence of government is control, or the attempt to control. He who attempts to control another is a governor, an aggressor, an invader; and the nature of such invasion is not changed, whether it is made by one man upon another man, after the manner of the ordinary criminal, or by one man upon all other men, after the manner of an absolute monarch, or by all other men upon one man, after the manner of a modern democracy.

What, then, should be the proper relationship between society at large and the individual?

The history of humanity has been largely one long and gradual discovery of the fact that the individual is the gainer by society exactly in proportion as society is free, and of the law that the condition of a permanent and harmonious society is the greatest amount of individual liberty compatible with equality of liberty. The average man of each new generation has said to himself more clearly and consciously than his predecessor: "My neighbor is not my enemy, but my friend, and I am his, if we would but mutually recognize the fact. . . . Why can we not agree to let each live his own life, neither of us transgressing the limit that separates our individualities?"

He called this reasoning the "real social contract," but disagreed with Rousseau that it was the origin of society; rather, he considered it to be "the outcome of a long social experience."

Throughout the 1840s and 1850s Stephen P. Andrews was a persistent opponent of racial slavery and an advocate of a theory which he called "the Sovereignty of the Individual." In his book, *The Science of Society*, he writes about the law of Individuality:

Individuality is the essential law of order. This is true throughout the universe. When every individual particle of matter obeys the law of its own attraction, and comes into that precise position, and moves in that precise direction, which its own inherent individualities demand, the harmony of the spheres is evolved. . . . Every scheme or arrangement which is based upon the principle of thwarting the inherent affinities of the individual monads which compose any system or organism is essentially vicious, and the organization is false—a mere bundle of revolutionary and antagonistic atoms. . . .

He then makes a distinction between individual freedom and individual license:

What, then, constitutes the boundaries of one's own dominions? . . . The limitation is this: every individual is the rightful Sovereign over his own conduct in all things, whenever, and just so far as, the consequences of his conduct can be assumed by himself. . . . *"The Sovereignty of the Individual is to be exercised at his own cost. . . ."*

It results from this analysis that, wherever such circumstances exist that a person cannot exercise his own Individuality and Sovereignty without throwing the "cost," or burden, of his actions upon others, the principle has so far to be compromised. . . . The unfolding of . . . Individuality is gradual, and its growing development is precisely marked, by the increase of its ability to assume the consequences of its own acts.

(For instance, in the case of a child, individuality must be disciplined until such time as reason has taught him to respect the individual rights of others. Likewise, an irresponsible adult must be restrained from interfering with the rights of his neighbors— hence, the necessity for courts of arbitration and police protection.)

Among the leaders of the collectivist school of anarchy was Michael Bakunin who was able to stalemate Karl Marx in their competition for the loyalty of the International, thus establishing an enduring Bakuninist tradition in southern Europe. Indeed, Daniel Cohn-Bendit and other young European radicals are more in the tradition of Michael Bakunin than of the dictatorial Marxism of Lenin, Stalin, and Brezhnev. The central issue which divided Marx and Bakunin in the nineteenth century is the same one which separates totalitarian communists from left-wing anarchists today—namely the issue of state ownership and control as opposed to the anarcho-collectivist ideal of "spontaneous socialism."

Whether the notion of a spontaneous socialist instinct arising in society once government is overthrown is a tenable one or not is another question. A dialogue developed over this question between the champions of individualist anarchism and the anarcho-collectivists. The individualists accused the collectivists of utopian idealism and economic slavery and asserted that socialism could only be implemented through coercive means. The anarcho-socialists, on the other hand, contended that individualism was a result of oppressive statism and all men would learn to live and share as brothers once they were free to express their true natures. This issue will be covered in greater detail later. But the main concern in this chapter is the fact that the collectivist anarchists of the 1800s were, naïvely or not, advocates of spontaneous socialism, and stand in direct opposition, with the individualist anarchists, to the brutal state authoritarianism that exists today.

In *Marxism, Freedom and the State*, issued in 1950 from a collection of Bakunin's writings, Bakunin referred to Karl Marx as the Bismarck of socialism and summed up his own ideal in these words:

It is the triumph of humanity, it is the conquest and accomplishment of the full freedom and full development, material, intellectual and moral, of every individual, by the absolutely free and spontaneous organization of economic and social solidarity as completely as possible between all human beings living on the earth.

Then he directs a frontal assault on the policies of Marx:

Marx is not only a learned Socialist, he is also a very clever politician and an ardent patriot. Like Bismarck, though by somewhat different means, and like many other of his compatriots, Socialists or not, he wants the establishment of a great Germanic State for the glory of the German people and for the happiness and the voluntary, or enforced civilization of the world.

Conceding that there is a difference between Bismarck and Marx in the fact that the former was a

"Pomeranian, aristocratic, monarchical Junker" while Marx was a "democrat, an Authoritarian Socialist, and a Republican," Bakunin then makes the point:

Let us now see what unites them. *It is the out and out cult of the State* . . . [Marx] loves government to such a degree that he even wanted to institute one in the International Workingmen's Association; and he worships power so much that he wanted to impose and still means today to impose his dictatorship on us. . . . The supreme objective of all his efforts, as is proclaimed to us by the fundamental statutes of his party in Germany, is the establishment of the great People's State (Volksstaat).

At this point many readers may want to ask themselves if Nazi Germany could have been possible *in exactly the same form* without the intellectual heritage of Karl Marx. How ludicrous is the *artificial* division between Left and Right when one considers that Hitler and Stalin were actually friendly enemies occupying the same bed. As Bakunin points out, the real distinction is not between opposing political slogans but rather between the fundamental question of liberty or a necessarily oppressive state:

. . . the first word of this emancipation can be none other than "Liberty," not that political, bourgeois liberty, so much approved and recommended as a preliminary object of conquest by Marx and his adherents, but *the great human liberty*, which, destroying all the dogmatic, metaphysical, political and juridical fetters by which everybody today is loaded down, will give to everybody, collectivities as well as individuals, full autonomy in their activities and their development, delivered once and for all from all inspectors, directors and guardians.

The second word of this emancipation is *solidarity*, not Marxian solidarity from above . . . but that solidarity which is on the contrary the confirmation and the realization of every liberty, having its origin not in any political law whatsoever, but in the inherent collective nature of man, in virtue of which no man is free if all the men who surround him and who exercise the least influence, direct or indirect, on his life are not so equally . . .

Peter Kropotkin based his theories of anarcho-communism on scientific discovery, believing that the data of biology, anthropology and history would eventually lead to the creation of a spontaneous, voluntary Communistic state. In *Revolutionary Pamphlets*, issued in 1927 from his essays, he writes:

The [scientific] anarchist thinker does not resort to metaphysical conceptions (like "natural rights," the "duties of the State," and so on) to establish what are, in his opinion, the best conditions for realizing the greatest happiness of humanity. . . . He studies society and tries to discover its *tendencies*, past and present, its growing needs, intellectual and economic, and in his ideal he merely points out in which direction evolution goes. He distinguishes between the real wants and tendencies of human aggregation and the accidents (want of knowledge, migration, wars, conquests) which have prevented these tendencies from being satisfied. And he concludes that the two most prominent, although often unconscious, tendencies throughout our history have been: first, a tendency towards integrating labor for the production of all riches in common, so as finally to render it impossible to discriminate the part of the common production due to the separate individual; and second, a tendency towards the fullest freedom of the individual in the prosecution of all aims, beneficial both for himself and for society at large . . .

Regarding the state:

. . . in a society where the distinction between capitalist and laborer has disappeared, there is no need of government; it would be an anachronism, a nuisance. Free workers would require a free organization, and this cannot have any other basis than free agreement and free cooperation, without sacrificing the autonomy of the individual to the all-pervading interference of the State. . . .

For a more updated version of anti-statist socialism we turn to Sam Weiner whose book, *Ethics and American Unionism*, published in 1958, took to task the union leaders of the 1930s for cooperating with Franklin D. Roosevelt and helping to create a vast welfarist bureaucracy:

In regulating the relations between the classes, the State increased its own power and the foundations of state capitalist "welfarism" were laid. The State could not have done this alone; it had to overcome the resistance of old-line capitalism and hence needed the cooperation of a mass labor movement in order to control the restless masses. The government of Franklin Delano Roosevelt enacted "favorable" labor legislation and gave the "progressive" labor leaders a chance to fill their treasuries with the dues and assessments of the newly organized workers.

Again:

The character and functions of the North American unions have changed greatly. A State-regulated economy needs a State-regulated labor movement. The government will help the unions so long as the leaders can assure the smooth cooperation of a docile labor force. The 'Welfare State' has come to assume ever-greater social functions and has intervened on an even-greater scale in the control of economic and social life. . . . Individual liberty and local initiative have diminished as the State domination of society has increased. The individual has had less and less to say about his own life and interests as the Government prescribes, to an ever greater degree, the conditions under which he must live. This process continues inexorably, regardless of the political party in power.

So we have come full cycle. The issue of capitalism vs. socialism is irreconcilable if one views it in terms of political control. For whenever appeals are addressed to a central governing agency, an all-powerful, all-pervasive authority with the power to take away and dispense favors according to the whim of the moment (usually dependent upon the results of the latest "public opinion poll"), the public will divide itself into two general camps and organize myriad lobby groups to pressure those in command for "favorable" legislation.

As we have seen after reviewing several writers of both capitalist and socialist schools of anarchy, they are united on the most crucial question of all: the absolute necessity for people to take control over their own lives, and the dismantling and final elimination of state authority over the life of man.

Their major disagreement is one of personal attitudes concerning the makeup of human nature itself. Will man, if left to his own devices, elect to live privately, trade his wits and talents on the open market, accept the fruits of his own labor and provide for his own happiness, and agree to relieve the misfortunes of those less talented than himself by voluntary means—or would he prefer to organize himself in voluntary communes, share the tools of production and the fruits of labor without angling for a larger proportionate share than his fellows, and live in a condition of spontaneous social communism? My own philosophical convictions rest with capitalism—not the hybrid, semifascist brand of state corporate capitalism that exists today, but genuinely competitive, unfettered, nonmonopolistic free-market enterprise that can exist only in a totally free society. It is a sad commentary that such a condition has never existed throughout the history of mankind—not even in the so-called "halcyon days" of freewheeling nineteenth century America with its racial slavery legalized by the state, state-owned postal services and state-regulated railroad industries. It is my opinion that man is basically capitalistic, primarily self-serving, but also immensely generous toward his less fortunate neighbors when he is permitted to live his life in peace. My rational commitment is to man the individualist, striving to attain his own happiness on earth, man as an end in himself, willing to rise or fall according to his own merits, with no moral claim on the life and property of any other individual.

Obviously, others disagree. Who is right? Is there any way of reconciling these two opposing views of human nature without resorting to violence, pressure politics, or deceit?

My answer is *yes!* There is. But only within the framework of anarchism.

And this is the subject of the next chapter.

FOUR

RADICAL DECENTRALIZATION:

An Anarchist Alternative

Power to the Neighborhoods . . . Achieve local control of Education, Housing, Sanitation, Parks and Police . . . Kiss off the Boredom of the Democratic Machine. . . .

Excerpt from the campaign literature of Norman Mailer and Jimmy Breslin during the New York mayoralty race, 1969.

Our campaign is based on the premise that we have been living under the delusion that government can solve the social problems of the people. Only the people can solve their own problems. . . . The neighborhoods have the right to control their own affairs.

Norman Mailer in a speech quoted in the *New York Times*, May 2, 1969.

In New York today, the face of the city, Manhattan, is proud and glittering. But Manhattan is not the city.

New York really is a sprawl of neighborhoods, which pile into one another. And it is down in the neighborhoods, down in the schools that are in the neighborhoods, where this city is cut and slashed and bleeding from someplace deep inside.

Jimmy Breslin in *New York*, May 5, 1969.

It is becoming increasingly apparent that if our cities are to function as healthy and dynamic organisms, responsive to the needs and desires of the myriad sectionalized groups which inhabit them, a drastic overhaul in current authoritarian urban government ought to be considered at once. Most of our major cities are more a collection of insulated villages and neighborhood complexes than they are cohesive urban units. This being the case, it follows that the interests of these diverse mini-societies will be in constant conflict with each other as long as they are governed by a central administration in City Hall. The present organization tends to create a multitude of lobby groups working at cross purposes in their efforts to obtain favors for their own particular communities. This abrasiveness in the structure of our cities produces friction and resentment and a series of explosive crises which erupt on the steps of City Hall with increasing frequency. There are too many diverse, antagonistic elements in our cities for the interests of all the people to be served by one central administration.

We have "conservative" neighborhoods, "liberal" neighborhoods, low-income neighborhoods, high-income and middle-income neighborhoods, black, Spanish, Jewish, Italian neighborhoods, and so on, seemingly to infinity. The question remains of what can be done about the organic structure of our urban areas to make them more palatable and more workable for the many groups that live there. Let us begin with New York City as a case in point, since virtually every large metropolitan area in the country faces the same problems in varying degrees.

It has already been suggested that New York be divided into five cities, each of the five boroughs becoming autonomous and self-governing. But this is not enough. We would still be left with five mammoth, unwieldy metropolitan areas averaging almost two million citizens each. This would not be nearly enough to defuse the explosive situation that now exists. The breakdown must be more ruthless, more complete if it is to work at all.

Paul Goodman has been speaking in terms of voluntary, community-centered urban life for more than thirty years. He has repeatedly refused to call himself a "liberal" because of the authoritarian welfare-statism that characterizes the liberalism of the twentieth century. As far back as the late 1930s, he sensed that there was something wrong with a philosophy which, in effect, calls for the creation of a powerful centralized bureaucracy in order to force people to live according to the life style dictated by subsidized teams of "pragmatic" social engineers. He developed the idea of small, voluntary, self-governing communities within our cities and referred to his plan as an anarchist alternative in order to differentiate it clearly from the left-wing liberalism of the day. His own brand of leftism has been labeled left-wing *libertarianism*, and he, himself, has been referred to as an anarcho-libertarian, an anarcho-liberal, a left-wing anarchist, and several other names by supporters and critics along the political spectrum.

Norman Mailer calling himself a liberal conservative during the New York mayoralty race of 1969, advocated a decentralization plan that was strikingly similar to the community-centered anarchism of Paul Goodman. Sensing something of both a conservative (neighborhood control, local self-help) and liberal (cooperative efforts for social equality, concern for justice in dealing with minority groups) nature in his proposals, he was apparently at a loss to define on which side of the political center he actually was. Without realizing it, he was endorsing a policy of consistent libertarianism which is neither of the modern left nor of the modern right, but rather militantly anti-statist and therefore anarchistic in its fundamentals.

Perhaps the greatest lesson to be learned from this is that left-wing *liberalism* and right-wing *conservatism* are basically irreconcilable because they are both statist in their essentials. As long as liberals speak of using the power of the state to "make men free," and conservatives speak in terms of police power to preserve the "moral climate of the nation," both sides will be locked in an endless tug of war to elect their own authoritarians into office and suppress the opposition. As long as we think in terms of politics and government to resolve our

differences, we will always be a divided nation with
various factions lobbying for "favorable" legislation
and a greater kickback from Washington to meet
the needs of each particular section of the country.

The Left and Right can be harmonized only
under anarchy. This becomes more apparent if we
think of the political spectrum as a circle rather
than a straight line. (See diagram on pages 44-45.)

As we study the diagram we see that the center
area at the top is a predominantly gray zone, a mixed
economy with its natural by-product, welfarism. As
we move toward both the left and right we enter an
area of stronger government control of the economy, conservative state capitalism on the right,
liberal socialism on the left. Moving further to the
right, we enter an area of right-wing fascism with
nominal private enterprise but, in actuality, total
government *management* of the economy, suppression of opposition parties and censorship over all
media of communications. Likewise, as one moves
further down the left side of the political circle
there is total government *ownership* of the means of
production and distribution, suppression of all opposition and censorship again of the spoken and
written word. But as one moves further to both the
left and right, he moves further on the right to the
ideal of capitalism, and on the left to the *ideal* of
socialism. Here is the broad spectrum of libertarianism, of voluntarism in the intellectual, economic,
social, and spiritual life of society. It is only here,
without government restrictions of any kind, that
people can learn to resolve their own differences

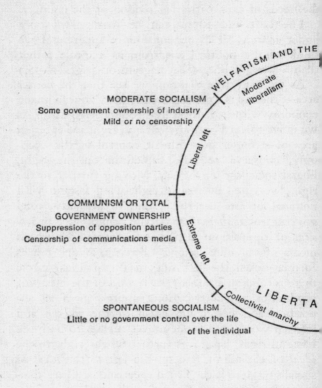

WELFARISM AND THE

Moderate
liberalism

MODERATE SOCIALISM
Some government ownership of industry
Mild or no censorship

Liberal left

**COMMUNISM OR TOTAL
GOVERNMENT OWNERSHIP**
Suppression of opposition parties
Censorship of communications media

Extreme left

LIBERTA

Collectivist anarchy

SPONTANEOUS SOCIALISM
Little or no government control over the life
of the individual

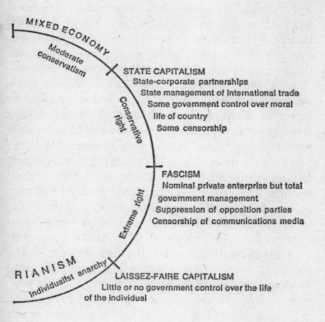

MIXED ECONOMY

Moderate
conservatism

STATE CAPITALISM
State-corporate partnerships
State management of international trade
Some government control over moral
life of country
Some censorship

Conservative
right

FASCISM
Nominal private enterprise but total
government management
Suppression of opposition parties
Censorship of communications media

Extreme right

RIANISM

Individualist anarchy

LAISSEZ-FAIRE CAPITALISM
Little or no government control over the life
of the individual

without resorting to the coercive powers of the state to suppress their opposition.

An interesting note to consider is that as one studies the diagram carefully, it becomes clear that the United States has been drifting slowly right-ward during the past thirty years or so, and not leftward as modern conservatives would have us believe. That is, we have been edging toward stronger and stronger government *management* of the economy, and not toward government *owner-ship*. When one considers the George Wallace phe-nomenon of 1968, there is no question that he, if he had been elected, would have moved the country from its present position between a mixed economy and state capitalism (with some government con-trol over the moral life of the country) toward open fascism with total government management and stronger censorship over the intellectual life of the nation. In part, this rightward trend in American politics accounts for the fact that today's conserva-tives are far more ardent defenders of the status quo (witness their hysteria over the Law-and-Order is-sue) than even the moderate left-of-center liberals. Moderate conservatives have far more to lose in our current struggle than any other faction in society.

It is evident that all of our Presidents from Franklin Delano Roosevelt to Richard Milhouse Nixon were, without exception, men of the center, with FDR, Truman, Kennedy and Johnson appear-ing slightly to the left of exact center, and Eisen-hower and Nixon slightly to the right because of their emphasis on "balancing the budget." It is interesting to speculate where Barry Goldwater would have taken us had he been elected President in 1964. Contrary to public opinion, it is most likely that he would have pushed the nation, not into the extreme right, but beyond that slightly into the libertarian section on the right. Recently, however, he seems to have abandoned his eccentric libertarianism of the early 1960s and now endorses the centrist policies of Richard Nixon. (See Karl Hess's "Open Letter to Goldwater," *Ramparts*, October, 1969.)

Also it becomes apparent that the Czechoslovakian struggle against Russia represents a desire to move beyond the extreme left-wing totalitarianism of state communism into the socialist ideal of libertarian socialism further to the left. May writers have speculated that the student/worker unrest in Czechoslovakia was a capitalist uprising. This is not so. Most Czechoslovakian intellectuals who have written on the subject maintain that the student/worker coalition in their country is still Marxist-oriented, and that their thrust was further to the left toward voluntary socialism. As we again see from the diagram, had they been permitted to drive relentlessly leftward, perhaps they would have entered the realm of anarcho-capitalism within the framework of a totally free society. Unfortunately because of the Russian intervention, these questions must remain, for the time being, mere speculation.

We might do well to ask ourselves if the United States government really wanted the Czechoslovakians to succeed in their uprising against their

Russian masters. Would greater freedom in Czechoslovakia really work to the best interests of the
power brokers in Washington, D.C.? With this
country strongly regulated from the top and capitalist in name only, is not an attack on Russian he-
gemony also a threat to the political machinery of
the United States? Could our politicians afford to
have American citizens witnessing an anarcho-libertarian revolution in Europe without exposing themselves to the same threat here? This is not to say
that the Johnson administration consciously desired
the destruction of freedom in Czechoslovakia—or
that the Eisenhower government was overtly pleased
by the rape of Hungary in 1956. But, since politicians are wielders of an incredible amount of power
over the life of the average citizen, it is impossible
to imagine them not experiencing some faint ripple
of panic over the spectacle of angry students and
workers shaking their own establishment to the
core.

So we see how Paul Goodman, labeling himself
a left-wing anarchist, and Norman Mailer, referring
to himself on the spur of the moment as a liberal
conservative, can arrive at essentially the same position. They are both operating within the lower
quadrant of the political circle. They are both
speaking in terms of libertarian, anti-state alternatives. They have struck upon a basic tenet of anarchist philosophy—radical decentralization.

Using New York as our model city, the metropolitan area must be subdivided into voluntary,

fully-autonomous neighborhood communities for the purpose of establishing complete local control over their own educational, police, sanitation, fire prevention, health, and economic relief systems. Each neighborhood community, small towns and villages unto themselves, should be permitted to re-organize themselves along the lines of their natural boundaries.

As an example, the upper westside of Manhattan is a loosely-knit community composed of a number of families and individuals with generally homoge-neous interests, all of whom, for various reasons, en-joy the tolerant atmosphere and style of life that is available to them in that particular village. It is a thoroughly integrated community with upper-mid-dle-income Jews predominating along Riverside Drive and West End Avenue; lower and lower-mid-dle-income blacks and Puerto Ricans along Amster-dam and Columbus; artists, actors and writers scat-tered throughout the side streets on either side of Broadway; smaller pockets of Cubans, Haitians, Dominican Republicans, and old Irish dotting the area between Broadway and Central Park West. It is also a haven for interracial couples who can live without being scrutinized and frowned upon by dis-criminating neighbors.

If the residents of this area feel any sense of loyalty to any particular geographical area, it is to their upper westside community and not to some amorphous, non-existent whole known as New York City at large. It is only natural that they would elect to participate in the life of their own village for the purpose of establishing the basic civic necessities.

This holds true for every other natural village in New York City consisting of a number of people with generally homogeneous interests, at least as far as their style of life is concerned. The people of Harlem, Inwood, Jackson Heights, Forest Hills, the East Village, and other neighborhoods throughout the city would undoubtedly elect to structure their own lives around their own particular communities. The only qualification here is that any such participation be of a voluntary nature if it is to be a truly anarchistic alternative to our present order. If an individual elects not to contribute to a particular service of the community he is then, of course, not entitled to share in the benefits.

Each neighborhood community would encourage the proliferation of privately-run schools on a competitive basis within the district. Some communities might decide to establish locally-controlled public school systems for those families that desired it and were willing to contribute toward the operation. Other neighborhoods might establish a combination of competing private schools and a community-public school if they thought that such a system would be more attuned to their own particular needs. Education on these lines would be relatively inexpensive compared with our current arrangement, and each family would be assured of the most relevant education for their children at the lowest available competitive prices. The motivation in each community, particularly in the ghettos, would be enhanced considerably if the local schools and curriculum were controlled by local private schoolmasters or a democatically elected community school board.

For the sake of effective education, if a school wanted to provide for twenty pupils per classroom, a school servicing 1000 pupils would require fifty teachers. Assuming their individual salaries averaged $8000 per year and that operating costs were $500 a month (which would be considerably reduced if the school owned its own property and was not obliged to pay coercive real estate taxes), the tuition per family would come to slightly more than $400 per year—approximately one-fourth the current cost of private education in New York, and a mere fraction of the several thousands a year per child that is now spent in our gigantic public school system. A school servicing a hundred students, with its drastically reduced overhead, works out to roughly the same cost per family.

Now these prices are almost negligible for the more affluent families in any given district, and they could be reduced even further for the poor through donations (which would be more readily abundant if people were not forced to pay coercive taxes), voluntary teaching by some of the more dedicated members of the teaching profession, and the formation of parent cooperatives such as now exist on a nursery school level to keep down the costs of administrative and maintenance personnel.

Certainly there is no utopian answer to the problems that now afflict our urban centers. Many unforeseen situations would be apt to arise, demanding imaginative thinking to avoid other crises. But there is no question that radical decentralization would drastically reduce the operating costs of our current educational system. "Decentralize! Decentralize!" ought to be the modern equivalent of Henry David Thoreau's admonition to "Simplify! Simplify!" Whatever obstacles did arise would be on an infinitely smaller scale than the mammoth, inhuman crises that are now an integral part of our daily lives. If we can reduce our big problems to a number of little ones, we would have a considerably greater chance of finding enduring, *nonpolitical* solutions for them.

Most likely each neighborhood community would elect to organize some sort of defense force to protect local residents from physical abuse and damage to property. Whether these would be voluntary neighborhood patrols or paid professional police forces would be solely up to the inhabitants of each particular community.

There is no question that our present police organizations, armed and controlled by centralized bureaucracies, sometimes behave like colonial troops in an occupied ghetto. We should recognize the need for police for what it actually is: a necessary evil which must be tolerated so long as men insist on initiating the use of force and violence against their neighbors. But most policemen today are not welcomed in the neighborhoods in which they serve because they are not considered to be defenders of the people. Rather, they have built a reputation as oppressors, extorting free meals from local restaurants and coffee shop owners, monthly handouts from proprietors of neighborhood ginmills, discounts on purchases from local shopkeepers, and collectors of graft from petty criminals whom they are supposed to be protecting the people from in the first place.

Local control over the police would change all this. As residents of the areas which they served, recognized as friends and neighbors by the local citizenry, policemen would be more conscientious about preserving life and property in their own communities. Today most policemen who do their tour of duty in the ghetto are contemptuous of the people they are supposed to serve and escape to their homes in the suburbs after work. What motivation have they to be conscientious in the performance of primary duties? With few exceptions they do not know the people, very rarely do they have to live with them, and there is no need at all to be responsive to their needs. With a police force drawn from the residents of the community, most rational people would be anxious to contribute voluntarily toward their own defense.

Figuring on one policeman for every 400 citizens, which is the ratio currently existing in New York City, a community of 40,000 people would require 100 policemen in order to be adequately protected. (If the police were confined to their proper duties,

protection of life and property, this ratio could be
vastly reduced. It is estimated that seventy percent
of a policeman's duties in New York City is of an
improper nature: busting kids for smoking marijuana, enforcing immoral obscenity and abortion
laws and other anti-sex legislation, rounding up
draft evaders who are defending their lives against
the state, breaking up peaceful demonstrations, etc.)
If each policeman earned an average of $8,000 per
year, the cost for 15,000 wage earners and approximately 1000 tradesmen and merchants servicing
the community would come to less than a dollar a
week to cover their salaries. Equipping them with
uniforms and weapons and allowing for fringe
benefits might bring the cost to slightly more than
a dollar a week for each contributor. When one
considers that landlords and merchants would most
likely pay a greater proportionate share because of
their greater exposure to property loss, the cost for
families would be even less. Tenants in apartment
buildings might not even be aware they were paying
for police services since landlords would probably
sign a contract to protect their property and work
in the premium as part of the rent. Each tenant
would benefit equally, and by sharing the cost with
the landlord and other tenants the cost for each
family would be almost negligible. We must also
remember that the $8,000 salaries we have been
talking about for teachers and policemen would be
worth far more than they currently are under our
inflationary system of wasteful government spend-
ing and coercive taxation.

At this point, some readers may object: doesn't all this smell of vigilantism? Wouldn't small neighborhood police patrols, unregulated by some central authority, be able to prey upon their own people? To this we answer that the present impersonal and centralized police departments are far more capable of preying on the public and getting away with it, and in fact are doing it today on no small scale. But a neighborhood force consisting of local residents would be far less likely to take advantage of their own neighbors. Grafters and extorters could be caught and weeded out much more efficiently under the watchful eye of a small community with total control than they are under our present system. Small towns *outside* the cities manage their police and keep them relatively honest with little or no effort. There is no reason to believe that small towns *within* the cities could not do equally as well.

Again, what if people refused to contribute *voluntarily* toward their own protection? To ask this question seriously one has to believe that people are so fundamentally irrational that they would prefer to be mugged, beaten, and have their property stolen than to pay the small amount it requires to organize a defense team. Wouldn't some people hold back? Probably some would. But again, on a neighborhood level, the moral pressure on a slacker who refused to contribute something toward a public defense fund would be so great that he would have to live virtually as a pariah in his own community. Certainly there would be a few diehard recalcitrants, but their number would be so small and their eccentricity so great that they are most likely presently living outside the mainstream of normal life anyway. The great majority of people, when they are permitted to live their lives as free, independent individuals, are fundamentally rational, cooperative and eager to get on as well as possible with those around them. It is only when force and pressure is used against people that they become obstinate and difficult to deal with. And there is no more coercive and oppressive force in the world than the power of government itself.

Small towns and communities have demonstrated that private garbage collection service is far more inexpensive than our present public system of waste, obsolescence, and featherbedding. Private companies motivated by the profit incentive are forced to keep overhead as low as possible in order to offer the best possible service at the lowest price and thereby beat out their competition. Private operatives cannot afford the luxury of obsolete equipment and nonproductive employees. They do not have the public "till" at their disposal and their income is directly dependent on the will of a fickle and demanding public. Like any other business concern, they must serve to please—or their customers, by giving their business to a more efficient competitor, will see to it that they do not serve at all. But a public sanitation system, enjoying a *coercive* monopoly in the garbage removal industry can allow waste, unproductiveness, obsolescence, featherbedding and general inefficiency to seep into its operation and the public is powerless to do anything about it. There are no competitors to which to turn.

Another way in which the public would benefit through the proliferation of competing private sanitation companies is in a better system of garbage disposal. Certainly no private company could get away for long with the current practice of "dumping" garbage at selected spots around the city. Competing companies would be forced to find better, more sanitary methods of getting rid of waste material. In certain parts of Europe garbage is refined and then used as land fill. There is a booming land fill market in this country and private garbage concerns might find a way to dispose of waste profitably and eliminate the pollution that now exists.

There is no question that Mafia domination of the limited private sanitation market in New York exists with the approval of government. The handful of private removal companies which service commercial enterprises in and around the city are operated and controlled by underworld figures. Politicians have known of this situation for more than a generation and have been filling their own pockets as a reward for permitting it to exist. This would not be tolerated on a completely open market. Without the assistance of government, the Mafia would have to declare war on the public itself in order to force its rule over an entire industry. With such violence brought into the open, gangsters whose identities are now concealed by the authoritarians they help elect to office would be exposed for everyone to see, and their organizations destroyed. Powerful underworld operations could have existed for as long as they have only with the direct assistance of government.

Private sanitation companies outside of New York City service the communities efficiently and satisfactorily for between one and three dollars a *month* per customer, depending on the population density of each community. Generally speaking, the heavier the concentration of people, the lower the cost. For most small communities in a large metropolitan area, the charge per family would be little more than nominal.

It has been suggested that such radical decentralization and dismantling of civic industries would not be possible because of the pensions and benefits that longtime civil servants have been building up over the years. But these critics overlook the fact that whole new industries would be born on the private market once these services were taken away from the state, and the experience and skill of present public employees would be in great demand by fledgling private companies. It is unfortunate that many of these employees have gotten used to the unrealistic situation of being able to retire at forty years of age with a guarantee of six and seven thousand dollars a year for the rest of their lives. Such a situation could only have been created by politicians with an unlimited claim on the earnings of the average citizen. If some of these men were forced out of "retirement" at forty-two years of age, after twenty years of service in the police or sanitation department, they could command good salaries as man-

gers and administrators for the new private enterprises. Originally, this "pension" money was stolen
by politicians from the average citizen without his
consent. If anyone has a moral claim to this money
it is the people from whom it was stolen in the first
place.

A private fire-fighting company in Arizona has
shown that it can provide better service for less than
one-third the cost of public fire prevention in a
community of equal size. With several private fire
prevention companies offering their services to a
community on a competitive basis, the public would
be assured of the most efficient service at the lowest
competitive prices. Public departments, again with
the public treasury at their disposal, can afford such
luxury as expensive brass ornaments adorning their
equipment. There may be some aesthetic value to
such ostentation, but it adds nothing to the operating efficiency of the Fire Department and is callously
wasteful of the taxpayers' confiscated money.

If the citizens of any particular community were
so inclined, they would have the option of creating
public facilities for each of the services we have been
discussing in this chapter. Anarchists do not deny
the right of any group of free individuals to band
together for whatever purposes they desire. As long
as such associations are voluntary and they do not
try to force their life style on others, or make them
contribute toward their voluntary collectives, they
have a perfect right to organize themselves in any
way they wish. This is the beauty of anarcho-lib-

ertarianism: utter and complete toleration for any
and all styles of life so long as they are voluntary
and nonaggressive in nature. Only under such a
system can the capitalist and socialist mentality co-
exist peacefully, without infringing on the rights of
other individuals and communities.

Dr. Thomas W. Matthew, founder of the National
Economic Growth and Reconstruction Organization (NEGRO), a black self-help organization, has
criticized the present welfare system as a "glorified
WPA for Negroes." The welfare state, according
to Dr. Matthew, has produced a black population of
"kept citizens" and is contributing toward the increasing frequency of riots in the black community.

Roy Innis, National Director of CORE, has repeatedly favored self-determination and an end to
"Mickey Mouse programs" that only perpetuate
Negro dependence on a paternalistic white government.

There is no question that the current welfare system is, by its nature, an act of condescension. In
New York City politicians have created a veritable
"welfare industry" operated and directed by political power brokers who have come to depend
on its existence as a cornerstone of their own power
structure. An army of workers has arisen whose
careers are an integral part of human misery. Do we
actually expect these people to eliminate the indigent
from the welfare rolls, to rehabilitate them and
prepare them for an independent role in life when
any reduction in the number of welfare recipients

necessarily means a diminution of their own job responsibilities? Do we expect them to put an end to their own careers? It is in their own interest to work for the enlargement and expansion of the welfare state, creating an even greater demand for their own peculiar talents.

Along these same lines, it is also apparent that as the welfare rolls increase, with approximately one million people (one out of every eight New York City residents) now dependent on some sort of public dole in New York, their number represents a growing bloc of potential voters. Can any aspiring politician fail to ignore the political reality inherent in this fact?

As the rolls increase, as more and more of the nation's poor come to depend on the machination and "benevolence" of their patronizing masters in City Hall, they will come to despise and resent these bureaucratic czars as perpetrators of their own dependency. Are we so naïve, have we become so jaded that we cannot see the potential fodder for revolution the politicians are creating in their insatiable lust for power? As neighbor turns on neighbor and the city burns, the politicians who have lined their pockets at the public's expense will depart for Bermuda and parts unknown until there is nothing left but the fragmented bits and pieces of a broken society.

It is time to redefine "welfare" in terms of its original concept: it is a *relief* system, a program for providing the indigent and temporarily unemployed with a means of subsistence until such time as they are able to take care of their own essential needs. There is nothing degrading in the prospect of a man who is down on his luck and requires some neighborly generosity to help him feed himself and his family and to meet his financial obligations. But there is something base and degenerate and obscene in the spectacle of political exploitation of human misery and suffering. Community control of all social relief agencies is the best way of eliminating individual fraud and keeping political exploitation of the poor to a bare minimum. Whether these would be privately run, in the sense of voluntary charitable organizations to which people could apply for help, or whether a community relief agency should be established depends, again, on each particular community.

Obviously, more affluent neighborhood communities such as the eastside of Manhattan and middle-income sections throughout the boroughs would have little or no need for any such relief agencies. It is only the Harlems, the Bedford-Stuyvesants, the South Bronxes, with their heavy concentration of low-income families, that depend so critically for survival on human generosity. Wouldn't it be a great boost to their self-esteem if they were to hold bazaars and lotteries and sell tickets within and outside their own communities, if they were to solicit voluntary contributions from the affluent instead of depending on coercive taxation for the funds? After taxes which today confiscate an average of over twenty percent of a man's paycheck, six cents on every dollar he spends for purchases, which penalize him for every improvement he makes on his own real estate, which comprise over half the cost of a bottle of liquor or a pack of cigarettes, or one-third the price of a gallon of gasoline—taxes, in sort, which inflate every penny of every dollar he spends for his own survival and pleasure so that his earnings are worth less in real value every month—there is very little room left for human generosity.

If we can only shuck government off the backs of the people, if we can rid our society of oppressive and exploitive politicians and all the restrictions they have put on the normal pattern of human intercourse, we might find the average person to be a far more generous animal than we customarily give him credit for.

Each neighborhood community might appoint its own board of administrators to supervise local operations for that community. Generally the closer the administration is to the individual citizen, the more likely he is to be satisfied with the way in which public moneys are spent. The organic structure of each community might vary greatly from neighborhood to neighborhood. Thus the East Village might take the shape of a sprawling love-in for pot-smoking dropouts; the upper westside a miniature bureaucratic welfare state with each family contributing voluntarily to community institutions; Harlem an individualist republic; Jackson Heights a book- and movie-censored, Law-and-Order garrison; Park Slope a cultural paradise for working writers and artists. Most importantly, participation in the life of any community would be strictly voluntary, and it would take its form according to the will of the local residents. Each citizen would be free to move to any community that was more attuned to his own philosophical convictions.

Further problems remain, of course. What do we do with health services, public libraries, housing agencies, departments of consumer affairs, water and air pollution, suicide prevention, and other agencies now in existence? Many of these services could be handled by private interest groups organized across community lines, or within communities by volunteer associations or district administrators. Or these services might be ignored entirely by communities which considered them unnecessary.

For instance, government throughout history has been totally ineffective in its responsibility to protect the individual from pollution of the environment. Would not a privately organized *economic boycott* be much more effective in penalizing guilty companies from creating industrial filth and automobile exhaust? Economic power—withholding the dollar from the products of offending companies— would work wonders in spurring industry toward finding more acceptable means of dumping waste materials or inspiring the auto makers to develop a cleaner exhaust system. The point should be made that most forms of pollution are a violation of property and human rights, and test cases to this effect are now being undertaken in various parts of the country. In the future we will see more emphasis placed on judicial means as a way of dealing with pollution. The public has been told for so long that government was going to clean up the air, the rivers, and the soil that it has been lulled into a state of apathy while the authorities accomplish little or nothing.

The same principle holds true in consumer affairs. We have been told that chain grocery stores and drugstores have been overcharging residents in the ghettos. But they cannot do this for long if the local people set up picket lines outside the stores of offending merchants or take their trade elsewhere, even outside the community if they have to. Before long, miserly tradesmen would feel the pinch and change to more equitable practices. In Harlem, a group of businessmen organized a peoples' cooperative grocery store to drive exploiting merchants out of business.

Let us consider the subject of rent controls. It is no accident that New York, the only major city in the United States to retain rent controls, is suffering from the most critical housing situation in the country. If the city administrators were to eliminate real estate taxes and throw the market open to the people, supply would eventually meet demand and everyone would be housed at the lowest available competitive prices. When one considers the overhead a property owner has in taxes alone, the minimum rent that he must charge merely to break even is raised considerably. But the subject of rent control has become a political football. It is a weapon that politicians have created to set the people against each other—tenants against landlords, poor against rich—while the politicians sit back smug and secure, growing more and more powerful as the people vent their rage on one another instead of the parasites in City Hall.

Public libraries could be replaced by private renting libraries, or community public libraries could be established and supported by those people who wanted to make use of them. If any group of individuals wanted to form a voluntary kibbutz complete with public health services, public housing, public commercial cooperatives, public education, equal sharing of property and profits, such is their absolute right as free men and women. Obviously, some people prefer a collective style of life and, as long as they do it voluntarily without forcing others to support them, there is no reason why they cannot "coexist" peacefully alongside their capitalistic neighbors. People could then compare differing life styles and perhaps adapt varying elements into their own way of life. But this type of peaceful coexistence is possible only under anarchy.

There are other areas to be considered here. Should automobiles, liquor stores, taverns, television and radio stations, etc., by licensed by the state? Should roads and sidewalks be owned by the state? My answer is *no!* All these things should not be. The subject of unlicensed automobiles and privately-owned roads and sidewalks is the substance of a separate volume in itself, and ought rightly to be covered as part of a general discussion of the meaning and practical application of the principles of unregulated, free market capitalism. Such an economic system has never existed throughout the entire history of man on earth. Nor has even a close approximation been attempted, despite all the talk we hear about "laissez-faire capitalism" in 19th century America. For a more detailed discussion on the nature of unregulated capitalism, I would refer readers to the writings of Murray Rothbard, Ludwig von Mises, Henry Hazlitt, and F. A. Harper for starters.

The main purpose here is to demonstrate the concept of radical decentralization as a viable alternative to our present centralized and chaotic system. It is to show how a bridge can be made between the individual and the collective, the socialist and the capitalist mentality, without resorting to force and coercion. Of course, not everyone will be satisfied with such an operation. But to these critics I ask, do you have anything better to offer? Can you suggest any other way in which the differences between Left and Right can be reconciled without resorting to force in order to make others live according to your own particular bias? Or do you prefer a continuation of the present state of undeclared war among the various factions of society until the very fabric of civilization itself is rent and torn and destroyed forever? People must begin to realize that the real enemy is *not* other people, but the state—the violent and oppressive nature of government itself. We have had enough of ideological posturing and clichés. If we do not sit down and work out our differences now, the precarious world in which we live will surely explode and destroy us all.

These principles we have discussed in relation to New York City could be applied just as readily to cities throughout the nation. They would probably be more immediately operable elsewhere as other cities are less complicated by size and ethnic diversity.

It might be argued that such a program would only further isolate the various groups that comprise the citizenry of the cities; it would build greater barriers between the blacks and whites, the rich and poor, the educated and undereducated. I do not think that this would be the case, any more than the citizens of New Rochelle can be said to be "isolated" from those of Mount Vernon because they do not share a common municipal administration. There is more reason to believe that the current lobbying for favors at City Hall is driving people further apart and that under decentralization the various groups would stop regarding one another as members of competing lobby organizations. Perhaps they could then learn to cooperate with each other as free and peace-loving neighbors. In addition, individuals always have the right to vote with their feet. The upper westside of Manhattan is proof that integration can work when it is voluntary; it is probably one of the most thoroughly integrated and exciting neighborhoods in the world. The competition among the various neighborhood communities would spur each district on to heights of greater performance. If things seem to be progressing well in another community, people who otherwise would never have dreamed of living there might be tempted to move in.

Centralization has failed on all levels of government: federal, state, and city. There is ample evidence that people are usually happier and more productive when they are permitted to exercise control over their own lives. The clamor that is now being raised throughout the country for decentralization, from intellectuals on both sides of the political spectrum, ought to be heeded. It ought to be heeded particularly at this time when there is such a universal demand for it.

A continuation of the present order will surely lead to further chaos.

FIVE

TOWARD A RATIONAL FOREIGN POLICY:

Defending the Nonstate

Libertarianism, unalloyed, is absolutely isolationist, in that it is absolutely opposed to the institutions of national government that are the only agencies on earth now able to wage war or intervene in foreign affairs.

From "The Death of Politics," by Karl Hess, *Playboy*, March 1969.

To commit the sparse ground forces of the non-Communist nations into a land war against this Communist land mass [Korea] would be a war without victory, a war without a successful political terminal . . . that would be the graveyard of millions of American boys. . . .

Herbert Hoover advocating American evacuation of Korea, December 1950.

America was born in a revolution against Western

imperialism, born as a haven of freedom against the tyrannies and despotism, the wars and intrigues of the old world. Yet we have allowed ourselves to sacrifice the American ideals of peace and freedom and anti-colonialism on the altar of a crusade to kill communists throughout the world; we have surrendered our libertarian birthright into the hands of those who yearn to restore the Golden Age of the Holy Inquisition. It is about time that we wake up and rise up to restore our heritage.

From "Confessions," by Murray N. Rothbard, *Ramparts*, June 15, 1968.

It should be no surprise to anyone that the United States of America, our beloved "haven of freedom against the tyrannies . . . and intrigues of the old world," is now a symbol of imperialism and aggression in every corner of the globe. The avalanche of invective directed against America imperialism is on a par with, and oftentimes even surpasses, the vitriol showered upon our arch rivals, the Soviet Union.

The 1950s were, if nothing else, a decade of apathy mingled with bewilderment. Americans had long cherished the image of their nation as a peace-loving, isolationist fortress which had to be dragged reluctantly into two world wars for the sake of preserving international harmony. Suddenly, rudely it seemed, we were stunned by the incomprehensible spectacle of an American vice-president, Richard Nixon, being spat upon and showered with abuse during a state tour through South America, and an American President, Dwight Eisenhower, being forced to cancel a visit to Japan because of violent anti-American demonstrations. How easy and convenient it was to blame it all on the Communist conspiracy. Surely there could be no other explanation. Was not the United States a "haven of freedom against the . . . intrigues of the old world," a peace-loving nation which would use its immense power only in defense of justice? Those who hated us and the ideals we represented must of necessity be opposed to peace, justice, freedom, and therefore were agents of a communist plot to enslave the world.

Then came the 1960s, the expansion and escalation of American and Soviet nuclear power, the new Asian ground war in Vietnam, and an outspoken generation of young Americans who began to challenge the pat assumptions of the previous decade. This generation of American youth told us that the United States, our peace-loving bastion of freedom, was imperialist; that the United States was an aggressor; that the United States of America was a colonialist power, oppressive, tyrannical, fascistic; in short, they told us that the U.S.A. was everything we hated and thought we were fighting against for the past two decades since World War II. It is a sad indictment of the American political establishment that its typical response has been to call for suppression of our youth, suffocation of dissent, and the use of armed, combat-ready troops to silence the best-educated, best-informed, most liberty-loving generation of Americans this country has seen since its earliest days.

The youth of this nation will not be silenced. The

student revolution has succeeded and is now succeeding in rattling the apparatus of the state as nothing has since the founding days of the American nation. Make no mistake about it—it is a revolution in the purest sense of the word: a long, continuing, gradually escalating opposition to offensive government institutions with the ultimate aim of destroying them (more on this in the next chapter). Whether it will succeed in its final goal, the creation of an open society free of coercive state institutions, or whether the confrontation will result in the creation of an undisguised, dictatorial fascist republic is not immediately apparent. The student rebellion in France succeeded in toppling a more advanced form of fascism than exists in this country, but then the French students enjoyed the benefit of a large measure of support from the productive middle class. The large American middle class, from the blue-collared construction worker to the white-collared Wall Street analyst, remains committed to the preservation of the corporate state and the continuation of its own vested interests in the political establishment. When twenty-five percent of the country's work force is directly employed by some apparatus of the state machinery and another sizeable proportion is largely dependent on government war contracts, it is understandable, if not commendable, that they are not enthusiastic about tampering with the status quo.

It must be obvious to anyone who cares to take the time to think long and carefully about the matter that there is definitely something tragically wrong with America's policy toward the rest of the world. The easy way out is to dismiss this current generation of young Americans as "unpatriotic rabble," as "Communist-inspired revolutionaries," as "un-American troublemakers" who ought to be dealt with "quickly and firmly." Many Americans take comfort in the notion that the great majority of our young are really "decent, law-abiding kids," and most of the trouble is caused by a "well-organized minority." But these critics fail to recognize the fact that, historically, most movements (including Christianity and the American Revolution) have been conceived and implemented by small bands of visionary radicals with a dream for a better and more just future world, and the present revolution is no exception. Just as the few visionaries of the past were able to convert an ever-expanding army of disciples to their cause, so today the "small, radical minority" is expanding into a full-scale grass roots youth movement. While many students have deplored the tactics of the rebels, the majority has always been in sympathy with their goals.

Perhaps it is time to sit back quietly and analyze the positions of these two broad, opposite camps—the concerned "anti-Communist" American middle, and the anti-militaristic American youth—and see what conclusion we can reach.

In an article appearing in *Human Events*, May 24, 1969, Phyllis Schlafly and Admiral Chester Ward ask the question: "Are the Soviets planning a nuclear first strike?" Their answer to this ominous question is a startling *yes:* all available evidence seems to indicate they are.

Before proceeding, it should be pointed out that Schlafly and Ward are not to be dismissed as members of the "know-nothing, lunatic right." Phyllis Schlafly is a Phi Beta Kappa with a Master's degree in political science from Radcliffe College, co-author with Admiral Ward of three best-selling books, and author of the 1964 best-seller, *A Choice Not An Echo*. Chester Ward was Judge Advocate General of the U.S. Navy from 1956 to 1960, and he now lectures on national strategy in seminars conducted by Stanford Research Institute, the Institute for National Strategy, and the University of Pennsylvania. In short both of them are people whose views ought to be given a serious hearing.

Their source of information, which convinced them that the Soviet Union is planning to devastate us with a surprise first-strike nuclear attack, was Soviet Colonel Oleg Penkovsky who, because of his access to top-secret Soviet files, must be regarded as the most important defector in history to come over to the West. According to the Schlafly-Ward account, Penkovsky handed over secret documents through a British intermediary which are now filed in the Pentagon. These documents, entitled the "Special Collection," were hidden by Robert S. McNamara because they did not coincide with his own plans to de-escalate the arms race and decimate the strategic striking power of the United States. The "Special Collection" is a detailed account of top secret Soviet plans proving explicitly that the Soviets intend to launch a nuclear attack upon the United States as soon as they are convinced that they can destroy our retaliatory capabilities. Most important, there is no evidence that President Nixon or Secretary of Defense Laird has seen these documents because of two critical factors: first, "the intelligence community, still in the hands of holdovers from the McNamara-JFK-LBJ Administration, does not speak up because to do so would expose years of being wrong," and second, "as far as the Armed Services are concerned, very few military men ever had access to the 'Special Collection.'"

How do Schlafly and Ward know the contents of the "Special Collection"? Colonel Oleg Penkovsky describes them in detail in his published diaries, *The Penkovsky Papers*. Phyllis Schlafly and Chester Ward quote the following excerpts:

A future war will begin with a sudden nuclear strike against the enemy. There will be no declaration of war. Quite to the contrary, an effort will be made to avoid a declaration of war. When conditions are favorable for delivering the first nuclear strike, the Soviet Union will deliver this strike under the pretense of defending itself from an aggressor. In this way it will seize the initiative.

All operational-strategic plans of a future war are being developed in this direction. This does not mean that the plans exclude so-called local wars; on the contrary, Khrushchev is for local wars as a prelude to a future "big" war for which intensive preparations are being made. . . ." [According to Penkovsky, these plans have not been changed since the time of Khrushchev.]

All the authors recognize the importance of the first thermonuclear strike. . . . It is important not only as far as the initial stage of the war is concerned, but also because it concerns the entire course and outcome of the war.

Secondly, strategic nuclear missiles, which will play a tremendous part in the initial state of the war, will also make it possible to achieve the necessary strategic goals of the war within the shortest possible time. . . .

The Soviet Union does not wish to wage a long war. The Soviet Union will not be able to achieve victory in a long war because the country's economy and the people's morale will not endure prolonged ordeals.

Penkovsky quotes a passage from an article written by Maj. Gen. M. Goryainov of the Engineering Technical Service, ending with the passage: "Victory by one side depends upon readiness and ability to finish the war in the shortest possible time."

Then Penkovsky returns to his own thoughts:

I fear this more every day. And my fears confirm my choice to make this invisible fight. In Moscow I have lived in a nuclear nightmare. I know the extent of their preparations. I know the poison of the new military doctrine, as outlined in the top-secret "Special Collection.". . . I know their new missiles and their warheads. I have described them to my friends. Imagine the horror of a 50-megaton bomb with an explosive force almost twice what one expects. They congratulated themselves on this.

I must defeat these men. They are destroying the Russian people. I will defeat them with my allies, my new friends. God will help us in this great and important work.

He capsules the Soviet strategic doctrine with the words: "The plan to strike first, at any cost."

Schlafly and Ward go on to chronicle Soviet weapons development over the past ten years, attempting to demonstrate that they are tailor-made to carry out the Russian plan for a first-strike attack on the United States.

Now these are serious thoughts, and before we attempt to analyze them, let us turn to a speech made in Washington, D.C. on March 17, 1969, by Democratic Senator Henry M. Jackson, of the state of Washington. According to Senator Jackson we are living under five dangerous delusions at present.

The first is the myth that "the Soviets are on a fixed course toward more peaceful and moderate policies, and are ready to leave their neighbors alone." Senator Jackson believes that the truth is just the opposite. As proof he cites the Russian invasion of Czechoslovakia, their development of a Fractional Orbital Bombardment System, the production of Polaris-type nuclear submarines, and the expansion of Soviet naval activity.

The second myth is that "the Soviet rulers are becoming progressively more liberal and civil rights conscious, and are about ready to rejoin Western society." As a refutation of this thesis he mentions the war on Russian intellectuals, the attacks on Jewish authors and poets, the refurbishing of Stalin's image, and other shifts toward "hard-liners" in the Soviet Politburo.

Myth number three is the idea that "it is the United States that is heating up the arms buildup." Senator Jackson states that it was the Russians who "acted first to develop long-range intercontinental surface-to-surface missiles"; the Russians who "acted first to test-fire an ABM against an incoming nuclear-armed missile (in 1962) and they are the only nation to have done this"; the Russians who "acted first to develop and deploy a Fractional Orbital Bombardment System (FOBS), a first-strike oriented weapon . . ."; and the Russians who "acted first to deploy an ABM. . . ."

The fourth delusion is "the notion in some quarters that the only way to manage our problems with the Soviet Union is 'instant negotiation.' " This is "silly" says Senator Jackson because oftentimes negotiations are, for the Soviet Union, a method of "buying time to build up its own military forces, or of bringing a sense of relaxation and goodwill before instigating some energetic offensive on a new front." There is only one "safe way" to bargain with Moscow, and that is from a position of strength.

The fifth and final myth is "the latest version of the devil theory of history" conjured up in the spectre of the "military-industrial complex." For Marx the devil was the capitalist; for Hitler it was the Jew; and for modern appeasers it is the military-industrial complex. Senator Jackson claims it is the Russians who compel us to spend so much on national defense because they started the Cold War and are continuing to escalate the arms race. Obviously, in this country we must "rely mainly on private industry to do most of the research and build most of the new weapons system needed for national defense."

For the sake of discussion and in order to grant as much leeway as possible to the position of the "anti-Communists," * let us accept the arguments put forth by Phyllis Schlafly and Chester Ward, and by Senator Henry M. Jackson. Let us accept their indictment of Soviet hostility, aggression, militarism, and even the charge that the Soviet strategists are now hell-bent on a plan to destroy us with a first-strike nuclear attack.

But, for the sake of balance, let us now pose the following questions:

Which nation was it that first made use of atomic weapons against another power?

Which nation was it that first began to stockpile an arsenal of nuclear warheads?

Which nation was it that, until recent times, enjoyed a commanding lead in nuclear striking capabilities over all other nations, or combination of nations?

Which nation was it that first constructed a submarine capable of firing nuclear warheads?

---

* By this I do not mean to imply that all others are not against communism. A Libertarian is, of necessity, opposed to all forms of tyranny. But "anti-Communist" has come to be used as a term describing proponents of the ABM and other aspects of the arms buildup.

Which nation is it today that encircles the earth with nuclear rocket launching sites capable of striking any and every cranny of the globe?

The answer to all these questions, sadly, is the United States of America. It is not enough to say that we only did this as a defense measure. We did drop the first atomic bomb, the effects of which are still being felt today and, as far as we know, will continue to be felt well into the future.

It is not enough to say that we have always been a peace-loving nation interested only in defense. Our wars against Mexico, Spain, Korea, and Vietnam were not defensive as far as the territorial integrity of the United States is concerned. It was American generals who advocated, quite seriously if we are to believe the various accounts on the subject, "preventive war" against Communist China to guard against their "future potential."

Anyone who has ever seen a map of the world detailing the positions of American nuclear striking power must shrivel in horror at the prospect of the Soviet Union encircling us in the same way. Yet we expect the Russians to accept our explanation that such ubiquitous deployment of hellish weapons was undertaken solely in the interests of defense.

The United States was the first to assemble the most prodigious and horrific war machinery known during the entire history of man on earth. Did we accomplish this solely because we wished to deter aggressive Russian designs on the rest of the semi-free western world? Certainly this was a key factor in our initial decision to stockpile atomic weapons, but there is ample evidence that President Harry S Truman also attempted to use our radioactive muscle in an attempt to gain greater concessions from our wartime ally, Josef Stalin. And Harry Truman was the man who had already ordered atomic bombs dropped on a less formidable power than the Soviet Union.

So it appears that just as paranoia exists on both the Left and Right in our own political spectrum, there is an even greater element of paranoia entering into decisions affecting the international political arena. We began to develop atomic and then nuclear weapons and deployed them around the world —largely because we were afraid of what the Russians might do to us if they only had the chance. It is equally apparent that Russia's creation of her own nuclear arsenal—and even her plan to devastate us with a surprise attack if such a plan exists—was done because of the equally chilling spectacle of finding herself girdled in a nuclear stranglehold by a nation that has already used atomic weapons. If Russia is intending to strike us a first nuclear blow, there can be only one logical explanation for it: fear, panic, near hysteria—the same kind of hysteria that prompted American generals to urge a "preventive" war against China, the same kind of panic that induces publications such as *Human Events* to urge further escalation of the arms race at any and all costs.

Do we actually believe that anyone would wish to reduce us to a radioactive desert simply to conquer us? What kind of madness is this? What would

anyone have to gain? In the first place, no con-
quering power would be able to inhabit us if our
air were radioactive. Second, the job of cleaning up
our streets and rebuilding our cities would be an
impossible drain on an already moribund Russian
economy. If the Soviet Union did destroy our cities
and the millions of people inhabiting them, there
would be nothing worthwhile left for anyone to
take over. We must conclude from this that any
Russian plan to deal us a crippling, first-strike nuclear blow is a plan motivated by hysteria. We already know the amount of fear and hysteria prev-
alent in our own country. It is a historical fact that
the most dictatorial, authoritarian, and closed societies are also the most paranoiac. Accepting this, it
must be apparent that the hysteria gripping the
Soviet Union must surpass our own, even to the
point of insanity. It is a tragic commentary that as
our own society grows more and more closed—and
we have been moving more in the direction of fascism than we have toward freedom—the hysteria
in our own country may mount to the point where
we, too, begin to think in terms of a "preventive"
first-strike attack on Soviet Russia.

Where will it all end? If both sides remain committed to the arms race, to fear and panic, to hysteria rather than reason, it must inevitably end in
confrontation—final and conclusive confrontation.

How can such a confrontation be avoided? One
side must begin, and begin now, to eliminate the
element which triggered the Cold War in the first
place: paranoia. In other words, one side must begin

to withdraw and dismantle some of its weapons. With each side possessing fifty and a hundred times overkill, there is surely ample room for maneuvering by both sides without either party being left undefended. What place do napalm, poison gas, poison chemicals, and poison bacteria have in an arsenal of defense in an age of nuclear weapons? Is it necessary to have them just because the other side possesses them? Is not a nuclear warhead enough of a deterrent against aggression? Must we match every hellish, anti-life contraption that is conjured up by a potential enemy?

At the risk of bringing charges of "traitor!", "appeaser!", "sell-out!" crashing on my head by conservative friends on the Right, I am going to state openly and sincerely that the United States can be a *more* secure, *better* protected "bastion of freedom" against any form of international aggression with one-tenth, or even one-fiftieth the power we now possess. The mere existence of a super-powerful, ubiquitous American nation is largely responsible for the fever of frantic anti-Americanism that has gripped most of the world for the past fifteen years. The best part of our American heritage, the hunger for freedom and anti-colonialism that gave birth to this nation, would be more readily visible for all to see if our military posture was made less visible and we threw open the floodgates of free trade with all the peoples of the earth. What a gesture for liberty, what a blow to all the tyrannies of the world would be dealt by the spectacle of a fearless and confident America willing to defend its own borders, but willing at the same time to trade its ideas and products and skills and know-how in the market places of the world.

How can any arsenal of Soviet or Chinese weapons combat a performance such as that? But if they tried? With guns? With bombs? A freer, nonaggressive America would be able to rally the considerable force of world opinion to its side in any confrontation with a hostile communist nation. But if they persisted? Would an open, anarchistic nonstate have the physical power to resist?

National governments are the only agencies on earth capable of waging wars. It is a cliché, but it is nevertheless the truth, that people do not start wars, only governments do. My thesis is that *the legal monopoly on the use of force and weapons of defense should be taken away from the state.* As long as the weapons monopoly remains in the hands of paranoid generals and politicians in Washington, the threat of war will always be imminent.

Here we are entering the area which separates the classical liberal from the free market anarchist. The classical liberal maintains that a state should be formed for the *exclusive* purpose of protecting life and property and preserving order. In concrete terms this includes a national defense force to protect the country from international aggression, local police establishments to defend the individual from domestic violence, and a system of law courts to arbitrate disputes among the various citizens. The anarchist says that government is not required even for these minimal functions—that government, even "limited" government, is by its very nature self-aggrandizing and will gradually erode the liberty of the people while simultaneously strengthening its own power. The anarchist realizes that once a "congress" or a "parliament" is permitted to exist, the politicians who preside there will not content themselves with "limited" functions, and once the war machinery is monopolized in the hands of generals and civilian war "experts," there is very little to prevent them from engaging in military adventures such as we have witnessed in Korea and Vietnam.

The anarchist is a natural enemy of any and all states at any and all levels of their operations. What about defense? The anarchist says let *the free market provide for its own defense*.

Just as a need for milk in a free society gives birth to competing milk companies which rise to supply the demand, just as a need for housing triggers the proliferation of building contractors competing to best fulfill the demands of the people, so a need for defense will be met by competing defense corporations selling their services to various communities. We now have a number of private corporations building war machinery and doing war research for the federal government. Under our present system the state acts as a middleman, taking money from the people and handing it over to the war industry after, of course, taking a percentage for itself to meet its padded, inflationary payrolls. Why not eliminate the middleman? Why cannot companies A, B, C, D, E, F, and G approach each community directly on a supplier-to-customer basis, each supplier detailing the defense services it has to offer for X amount of dollars per year? Industry can build airplanes, naval vessels, rockets, and can even hire ground forces. Why should they not control them also, strictly for defensive purposes?

Currently there is nothing to induce government to use its weaponry strictly in the interests of defense. This would not be the case with competing private defense corporations. Business is guided by a very demanding taskmaster: the profit motive. If community 1 signs a two-year defense contract with company F, and company F does not live up to its contractual agreements, community 1 can give its next contract to company B. It is therefore in the interests of company F to fulfill the letter of its contract as efficiently as possible.

But, some critics will ask, what is to prevent community 1 from hiring company F to attack and conquer community 2? Simply the fact that company F also depends for its survival on contracts with communities 5, 7, 13, 16, and 19—and perhaps, in a totally free market, on contracts with other countries scattered throughout the world—and anything company F does to weaken its own reputation as a reliable *defense* company will lose it business elsewhere. We can envision a situation where company F might have contracts to defend, not only various sections of the United States, but also sections of Italy, Israel, Egypt, Kenya, and Australia. Company B's contracts may be for other sections of the United States, as well as parts of Sweden, Germany, Japan, and so on. Is it not apparent that the risk of war would be reduced considerably under such a system of free-market defense? Even if other countries kept their "statehood," the United States would be well defended by her private defense corporations, and the risk of world war would be diminished in the absence of a ubiquitous American war machine.

Would such a system work perfectly? To answer this question affirmatively one would have to be a devout Utopian. Unfortunately, a perfect society depends on perfect individuals living within that society. Nothing on earth works perfectly at all times. It is the assertion here that the new system would be infinitely *superior* to the current one of aggressive nation-states embarked on a collision course which erupts in major wars every generation or so. In light of the past, the suggestion that a free market defense system might not be perfect becomes almost irrelevant. The fact that it might be even a little bit better than what we have now is reason enough to try it. Nothing could be worse than the state of imminent nuclear war which has existed on this earth for more than fifteen years.

Another benefit that a free market defense system would have for the people is the fact that it would be considerably less expensive than our present national system with its padded government payrolls, the development of inhuman, expensive weapons which *could not be used* without destroying civilization, the inflated government defense contracts which are inevitable whenever a supplier is not *directly* accountable to its customers, and the graft and exploitation which is an integral part of any political system.

What of our space program? Would not this be jettisoned without a federal government to loot the pocketbooks of taxpayers and pay for rocketships? If there is a demand for space travel and exploration —if some people want to go to the moon and beyond, and others want to see them get there—it is a safe assumption that some entrepreneur or groups of entrepreneurs will offer to supply the demand. Perhaps transportation companies, airlines and others, would offer excursion flights in the earliest days to those who wanted to pay for them. As the industry burgeoned, like any other industry which grows and expands its markets, its services would become less and less expensive. Perhaps the scientific community would solicit funds, pool its resources, and explore the stars solely for the advancement of its own and mankind's knowledge. Most important, the belabored lower and middle classes would not be coerced into supporting multi-billion-dollar adventures while still trying to provide their children with a properly balanced diet.

Would not the Russians then take a commanding lead in space exploration and reach the planets before we did? Possibly they would. There is no question, however, that Russia's space program is largely determined by our own race to space and the *military* implications that are inherent in any national space program. Most likely Russia, with its already strained economy, would welcome the chance to divert its own resources to more pressing domestic needs.

What if the Soviet Union pressed ahead anyway and built lunar rocket launching sites capable of destroying our cities? It is a historical fact that every weapon ever devised has prompted the creation of a defensive system capable of minimizing its impact. This would be a problem for our free market defense corporations to contend with and to discover reliable means of guarding against. Here again, in asking this question we must assume that Russia or any other potential enemy is willing to reduce us to a radioactive desert simply to conquer us, and that is, I think, an untenable assumption.

The most important aspect of free market defense is that the companies which are suppling defense services to the public depend on effective *defensive* operations for their own survival. Their profits depend directly upon the amount of peace and harmony they can guarantee to the various citizens of the world. With private defense corporations operating on an *international* level, they must do all they can to prevent hostile nations from attempting to conquer one another.

As for the argument that if they were too successful, that producing a climate of "too much" harmony in the world would eliminate the need for their own services, I think this proposition is baseless after careful analysis. If defense corporations were successful in reducing the danger of aggression, they would merely be reducing their own

overhead and would therefore be able to sell their
services less expensively to the public. It would *not*
affect their profit ratio. For example, if a supplier's
overhead is $100 per month, he must charge a cus-
tomer $110 a month to clear a ten percent profit.
But if he is "successful" and can reduce his own
overhead to $25 a month, he can charge as little as
$27.50 to make the same ten percent profit, or $35
to make his $10 monthly profit. The mechanics of
the competitive free market will determine the most
equitable cost as it is determined what the market
will bear for any services demanded by the people.
The notion that the public will be able to do away
with private defense corporations altogether is ab-
surd when one considers the original purpose of defense. In any given neighborhood of ten families,
even assuming that all of them were peace-loving
and nonviolent, each family would still want to
guarantee that its own life and property were protected *in the event* of future aggression. It is the
nature of any living, healthy, life-affirming organism to take at least minimal precaution to insure
its own survival.

Finally, could not private defense corporations
turn their arms against their own customers? Possibly they *could*. But government is also capable of
using guns against citizens of its own society; government is not only capable of doing this, but *is*, in
fact, doing it not only in Russia and other non-
democratic societies of the world, but even in our
so-called free and open American society. Government is using troopers armed with mace, truncheons,

and riot guns against dissenting students and frustrated minority groups. Government is using its legal monopoly on power to imprison any law-abiding citizen who refuses to be robbed in order to support such policies of the state as military adventurism or social welfare programs whether he believes in them or not. Free enterprise must go a long way to equal this brutality. Private defense corporations would be restrained by the strictest disciplinarian of all—the profit motive—from threatening force against the people. They depend on the continuing patronage of a happy and well-satisfied clientele for their very existence.

Is not all this talk about voluntary communities and an anarchistic nonstate merely idle theorizing and wishful thinking? If politicians are not going to give up power of their own accord, why bother to speculate on the nature of a free, open, noncoercive society?

Of course politicians will not freely relinquish their power over the public. It is rare for any individual or gang of power merchants to voluntarily put down the reins of even limited control, let alone the kind of mammoth authoritarianism that has been accumulated in Washington, D.C.

How, then, do people go about securing their own liberty? Here we enter the realm of libertarian strategy, and this is the subject for the following chapter.

THE LIBERTARIAN IMPERATIVE:

A Blueprint for Liberty

This country, with its institutions, belongs to the people who inhabit it. Whenever they shall grow weary of the existing government they can exercise their constitutional right of amending it, or their revolutionary right to dismember or overthrow it.

Abraham Lincoln, Inaugural Address, March 4, 1861.

Our present government protects certain political freedoms which make possible peaceful alterations of that government. This fact does not abrogate our right of revolution. . . . To say that I have no right to revolt against government coercion as long as freedom of speech and free elections exist, is to say that I have no right to violently restrain a burglar, so long as he is willing to converse with me on the ethics of burglaring while gathering up my silverware.

David Friedman, *The New Guard*, May, 1969.

The highwayman takes solely upon himself the responsibility, danger, and crime of his own act. He does not pretend that he has any rightful claim to your money, or that he intends to use it for your own benefit. . . . Furthermore, having taken your money, he leaves you, as you wish him to do. He does not persist in following you on the road, against your will; assuming to be your rightful "sovereign," on account of the "protection" he affords you. . . . In short, he does not, in addition to robbing you, attempt to make you either his dupe or his slave.

The proceedings of those robbers and murderers, who call themselves "The Government," are directly the opposite of those of the single highwayman.

From *No Treason* by Lysander Spooner.

Traditionally, libertarians have advocated purely intellectual means in their fight to achieve a laissez faire society. The power of ideas, the written and spoken word, coupled with the vote at election time, has long been considered the only acceptable way for rational men to accomplish a just order in society. This chapter will demonstrate that stronger, more militant methods can also be morally justified in terms of libertarian principles. They not only can but *must* be employed *now* if we are to achieve anything close to a true libertarian order within the next fifty years.

The fundamental principle involved here is that *every individual has the right to defend himself against any person or organization, including government, that initiates the use of force against him.* The right of revolution is inalienable; the right of revolution is nothing more nor less than the right of self-defense.

By revolution we do not necessarily mean to conjure the spectacle of armed struggle in the streets. Historically, revolution has taken many forms. In its mildest, most benign application it is accomplished by rebelling taxpayers who turn down a bond issue in a local referendum as part of a united attack on all state institutions. In its broadest sense, revolution is a continuing resistance by the people to offensive authoritarian institutions. The form such resistance should take at any given moment depends on a number of factors. Would intransigent opposition to government create even stiffer controls over the life of the individual? Would an actual overthrow of the existing order produce a more dictatorial regime in its place? Or would a properly motivated, properly organized struggle result in the desired goal of a freer and juster society for everyone?

The point here is that the people always have the right to defend themselves, the right to rebel. Exactly when and how they decided to avail themselves of this right is a more complicated question involving matters of practical consideration as well as intelligent strategy.

Most people are willing to submit to a certain measure of organized violence for the sake of harmony. In the United States the citizenry has ceded to the government the power of eminent domain— the brutal destruction of private property—for the sake of building a sleek and modern highway system or constructing high-rise public file cabinets to house the poor. They have even handed over their bodies to the state through the military draft in order to combat the "Communist menace." At times it appears there is no end to the indignities the people will accept in the sacrosanct name of government.

But there comes the time when coercion becomes unbearable. The argument that dissent through "legal" channels is the only acceptable means of rebelling is statist nonsense by which perpetrators of state authoritarianism are able to cow the public into submission. The Boston Tea Party was "illegal" and so was the American Revolution itself. The state can pass any laws it wants for the purpose of suppressing the individual. In many countries it is "illegal" to express or publish certain opinions. In sections of the United States it is "illegal" to kiss on the streets, and "illegal" for members of different races to join in matrimony. The fact that the state no longer bothers to enforce such laws does not make these laws less immoral and despicable. "Legality" was the excuse used by Nazis to defend their own cooperation with the state in the slaughtering of Jews.

The thesis here is that any law which violates an individual's natural right to the ownership of his own life and his own property is essentially unjust and immoral, and that the individual has a moral right to resist such laws. No one questions the right of a man to resist the violence of an armed mugger in the streets or the right of a shopkeeper to resist the attempts of an underworld organization to make him pay "protection money" (although in certain areas, including New York City, the right of an individual to protect himself from an intruder in his own home has been weakened by government —the same government whose primary function it is to protect him from violence in the first place).

Why, then, when a gang of looters and murderers is euphemistically labeled "government," does the average citizen cry out in alarm against an individual who fights to protect his own right to life, liberty, and the pursuit of happiness? The fact is that government, with its monopoly on the *legal* use of force, is unquestionably the most consistent violator of individual freedom that exists in the world today. It is government that forces peace-loving men into uniform and ships them halfway around the globe to kill-or-be-killed in a foul, uncivilized jungle; it is government that turns men into slaves on an average of nearly two days a week by confiscating part of their earnings through both direct and indirect methods; it is government that tears down a man's home for the purpose of constructing a super-highway or building a high-rise metal box. It is government that forces an overwhelming majority of the nation's youth into public schools and makes them study a curriculum their parents may not approve of, immorally condemns a woman to the agony of unwanted childbirth with brutal abortion laws, pokes an obtrusive nose into the bedrooms of consenting adults and calls them criminals, limits the profit a man can earn on his own property, penalizes the individual for improving his own real estate with escalating property taxes, and bullies, harasses, and torments the average citizen every time he tries to make a decision for himself.

Surely no Mafia, no Cosa Nostra, no gangland organization in the world has even begun to dream of such power.

This brings us to the next question: what methods should a rational libertarian employ in his fight for the right to control his own life as an individual?

It is no longer enough to wait patiently for the President to perhaps ease up on government intervention into the nation's economy—or to wait quietly for Congress to pass a watered-down version of an anti-draft bill which reserves for the President the power to reinstate a military call-up under "emergency" conditions (a guerrilla skirmish in northern Tibet may well be considered the next "national emergency"). The only effective way to rid our society totally and finally of government coercion (in addition, of course, to a ceaseless barrage of intellectual invective) is to confront offensive governmental institutions wherever and at whatever level they exist—to challenge them directly and to keep up a loud, well-publicized attack until they are dismantled.

The military draft must be regarded as the most brutal and unjust government institution in existence today. For here it is not a question of men's pocketbooks and property being plundered by government; life itself—existence, the most valuable gift man possesses, without which all other freedoms are impossible—is under direct attack. Libertarians should align themselves with draft resisters throughout the country. They should set up picket lines around the draft boards; lend encouragement and moral and physical support to all young men who decide not to be inducted.

Here we should comment on James Burnham's warning in *National Review* against "unprincipled alliances" with those who are protesting the draft as a way of weakening our war effort in Vietnam. Mr. Burnham, theoretically, is opposed to the draft system in principle, but he believes that an element of freedom must be sacrificed in the crusade to fight the "Communist menace" abroad. In answer to this position it should be first pointed out that it is not Mr. Burnham's freedom which is being sacrificed in order to carry on the war. It is one thing to talk about making personal sacrifices for a cause one believes in, and quite another to advocate sacrificing someone else's life against his wishes.

Second, as we have attempted to demonstrate in Chapter Five, there are far more effective means available to combat Communist expansionism abroad than the senseless destruction of thousands upon thousands of human lives. No one bothers to pretend anymore that we are fighting to preserve freedom in South Vietnam. The string of autocratic Saigon regimes represents a far greater form of tyranny than the village commune programs advanced by the NLF, and the defense of fascism in Saigon is a cause unworthy of the murder of a single American life let alone the forty-odd thousands that have already been lost.

The only "unprincipled alliance" that can be considered here is one which serves to strengthen the government's power to *nationalize* the youth of America and to perpetuate the inhuman slaughter and mindless folly in an area as remote from our own immediate concerns as any place could possibly be. Alongside a spectacle such as this, the threat posed by a few neurotic, pro-Communist students is infinitesimal.

Draft reform or anti-draft bills which give the President power to reinstate the draft during "emergencies" are not enough. Not until government openly acknowledges the fact that it has *no right* to forcibly induct free individuals into military service should libertarians be satisfied. An individual has the right to defend his life with a gun if necessary, but since the gun of the state is bigger, armed resistance seems highly impractical at this time. Other forms of resistance should be considered valid, including face-to-face confrontation with draft board officials and politicians who support the draft, the dissemination of anti-draft literature and ideas among the people, and the formation of anti-draft associations to aid all who are victimized by the system.

When the average American is compelled to work nearly two days a week for the so-called benefit of the "common good," it is clear that not only the income tax but the entire taxing mechanism of the state is perhaps the next most serious abridgment of individual freedom in our society. The time for a taxpayers' revolt is long overdue.

Libertarians should undertake a program designed to throttle the taxing power of government on federal, state, and city levels. Picketing of revenue offices is only the first step. Harassment techniques should be employed: refusal to file income tax forms combined with putting forms in the wrong envelopes; formation of anti-real estate tax committees, anti-sales tax associations, anti-liquor, cigarette, and gasoline tax organizations to make the voice of the people heard loud and strong, not only during election years, but at all times; lending moral and physical support to those under indictment for tax evasion; passing out anti-tax literature at revenue offices; organizing anti-tax groups on all levels of society, from the lower-income minority ghettos to the affluent suburbs, and coordinating their activities for common ends, and so on. With the pay-as-you-go system now in effect, it is admittedly more difficult to resist the power of government looters. But a well-organized program can throw a king-sized monkey wrench into this totally inhuman taxing machine.

There are incidents in various sections of the country—Wisconsin, New Jersey, Pennsylvania, Texas, Long Island—of successful attempts by taxpayers to keep their taxes from rising. In New Jersey and Pennsylvania landowners have banded together and are refusing to pay their real estate taxes; in Wisconsin and Long Island the voters have turned down an unprecedented number of school bond issues. This is a beginning. Hopefully, these successes are a prototype of things to come.

Groups of concerned citizens (not only women, as has been the case so far) should be organized to protest the brutal sex and abortion laws now on the books. Dozens of abortion and birth control clinics should be established throughout the country by private sponsors without regard to the law. Citizens should surround these centers arm-in-arm when they are threatened by invasion from armed henchmen of the state. Similarly, consenting adults ought to take up residence with each other, according to their own desires, without regard for civil marriage laws. Statutes forbidding interracial marriages should be treated as if they did not exist. It should be stated plainly that laws and licenses have no meaning in relation to the sexual lives of human beings. No authority in the world has the right to institutionalize the sex life of mankind. Sex habits are strictly the concern of the individuals involved, and libertarians ought to state this fact loudly and clearly.

As for the argument that society must maintain certain moral standards if it is to survive as a civilized entity, we can turn to a report appearing in *Time*, June 6, 1969. According to *Time*, sex crimes in Denmark have fallen off twenty-five percent since the legalization of pornography in that country. In addition, sales of "obscene" literature have dropped so drastically that "porno" shops are being driven out of business by the dozens. The ones that are still capable of making a profit are staying in business solely through the patronage of tourists—tourists from countries where pornography is illegal and who travel to Denmark out of curiosity. This is the best argument to date against the position that the state must legislate acceptable standards of morality if society is to remain civilized.

"You do not have the right to impose your moral or religious convictions on us," said Republican state senator, N. Lorraine Beebe of Michigan, according to a report published in the *New York Times,* June 13, 1969. She was protesting statements suggesting that abortion was tantamount to murder and denied the "civil rights" of unborn children.

"I am a woman who had a therapeutic abortion in a Catholic hospital," she continued, "and don't think I didn't come face to face with my conscience. But I never, never would have had the opportunity to have children if I didn't have this."

Federal licensing of radio and television stations is nothing more than a form of indirect and sometimes direct censorship over the communications media. The airwaves are to be considered property existing in nature, and radio frequencies and television channels belong rightfully to those who first pioneer them, much the same as land was claimed initially by the original homesteaders. The function of government in this case should have been nothing more than to acknowledge titles of ownership as each new frequency was claimed and to protect the property rights of each new pioneer and his heirs.

For years news analysts and presidents of the major networks have been yelping sanctimoniously about the lack of competition among big, government-favored business concerns. At the same time they have lobbied government for extension of their own exclusive "licenses" to operate, in effect adopting the same standards for themselves as those they are attacking. We pride ourselves on having "private" radio and television industries in this country, but they are private only in the sense that the radio and television sets which we purchase are our private property. The stuff that is piped into our livingrooms night after night is a mockery of free speech. The ideas and the standards of entertainment to which the American people are subjected are as much a product of the government as they would be under a dictatorship. If I put a gun to a man's head and tell him to be careful of what he says, his decision to censor his speech can hardly be considered voluntary. Likewise, Senator John O. Pastore's warning to the television industry against the airing of "offensive and suggestive" material was done merely under the guise of voluntarism. Implicit was the threat that government would do its own censoring if the networks did not comply.

We have arrived at the point where the Noxzema girl is said to represent a serious threat to the moral climate of the nation. And we accept this with a straight face instead of greeting the charge with the contempt and ridicule it deserves. Can there be any doubt that total government control of the broadcasting industry now looms as a dangerous threat over our society? It would be naïve to expect the brutish mentality of power politicians to stop with the Noxzema girl. The attack here is directed against the airing of all "offensive" material. Offensive to whom? Offensive to the public, of course. And who decides what is offensive to the public? The "experts" of our all-pervasive state, naturally. While the Noxzema girl is considered offensive by one expert one week, another week a different team of experts will regard certain political views as offensive. Whose political views? Maybe yours, maybe mine. It really makes no difference. The federal experts will certainly have reserved that decision for themselves.

If government continues its intrusion into the nation's broadcasting industry, it will unquestionably be only a matter of time before total control is attempted over the publishing business, the film industry, and virtually every other commercial channel of communications in the country. When this happens, when government has succeeded in destroying freedom of speech, freedom of expression —when it has, in effect, eliminated an effective *verbal opposition* to its own policies—we will then be witnessing the beginning of a genuine totalitarian regime and the final destruction of all pretense of liberty in the United States of America.

Libertarians should bet a high priority on their fight against government licensing of radio and television stations. The dangers we have outlined above should be brought loudly to the attention of the public. In addition, the czars of CBS, NBC, ABC, and so on, should not be acknowledged as the rightful operators of the channels and frequencies they monopolize through the courtesy of state power. "Pirate" stations, such as came into being off the coast of England, should be encouraged and supported whenever they appear.

The welfare industry is nothing more or less than a continuing act of robbery. The prime culprits are the politicians who do the actual stealing; those on the public dole, as recipients of stolen goods, are only secondarily responsible for the crime.

Unfortunately, many of those who are genuinely needy and incapable of providing for their own welfare have been co-opted into the system. Just as many people are forced to send their children to public rather than private schools because the very existence of a public school system has minimized competition among the private schools and rendered them more expensive than they would normally be under free market conditions, so a public welfare system has eliminated many possibilities for private charity that would otherwise be available in a totally free society. But many middle-income wage earners, most heavily victimized through coercive taxation in order to support the welfarist society, tend to shed their wrath on the welfare recipient instead of on the perpetrators of the system.

Libertarians ought to direct their main thrust at the politicians in their struggle to destroy the welfare state. The tactics used against the draft boards could also be employed at welfare centers. The dissemination of anti-welfare literature describing free market alternatives to welfare recipients might also be useful. Theoretically, the vote should be effective in turning out pro-welfarist candidates for office, but the overwhelming majority of today's politicians are more-or-less committed to the welfare state, and too often the public is forced to choose the lesser of two evils. Election *boycotts* might be effective if they could be organized on a sizeable scale—a refusal to vote for anyone along with a declaration that those abstaining regard the election as a calculated fraud and refuse to acknowledge the validity of the results.

These are the main issues which concern the true libertarian. There are other areas, extremely important but less publicized, which indicate how far we have to go in the struggle to achieve a laissez faire society. The licensing of automobiles and the airline industry, taverns and liquor stores, the drug and meat industry (competing consumer service organizations would be far more effective in protecting the public from abuses than are federal agencies such as the FDA), street vendors of frankfurters and cheap merchandise, household pets and guns and architects and psychiatrists and scores of trade and enterprises too numerous to mention should be ample proof to anyone that we are not living, despite prevailing propaganda, under a *free* enterprise economic system in the United States of America. To wage a campaign individually against every

single area of statist penetration now in existence
would take forever, and then some.

But the state cannot operate without politicians
and politicians cannot function without money. For
this reason, an *economic boycott* of the state is
perhaps the most powerful weapon that people can
employ in their efforts to rid their lives of the *legal*
looting and murdering that is now being undertaken in the name of government. The concerted
and organized withholding of tax revenues is the
biggest and most frightening stick that the large
American middle class can shake in the face of government. If such an operation can be properly organized and mobilized, the American people can
succeed in breaking the back of coercive government and conclusively rid our society of state intrusion into the life of the individual.

These methods may sound drastic and extreme to
many advocates of the libertarian philosophy. But
if they are not put into operation—and put into operation now—the libertarian dream of a free society
for each individual may well be destroyed while it
is still in its gestation period. If we are to realize
even a close approximation of libertarian justice
within our lifetimes, we must begin now to take a
more militant role in achieving it.

SEVEN

OPPORTUNITY FOR THE FUTURE:

The Time is Now

When do we begin?

There can be only one answer to the above question: immediately.

But, would not a libertarian revolution run the risk of bringing even stronger state controls over the life of the individual?

Yes, this is possible. But the state has been legislating progressively stronger controls anyway for the past fifty years or so *without* a concerted opposition to its policies on the part of the public. It should be apparent to everyone by now that passivity has failed as a deterrent to intrusive government; if anything, a docile citizenry has encouraged the arrogance of power-hungry politicians and sharpened their appetite for even stronger state authoritarianism.

If organized opposition to government should fail and result in a dictatorship, at least undisguised dictatorship would be more honest than our present shabby system in which we are, in effect, free to *elect* our dictators every few years. It would be less hypocritical if we could force our politicians to abandon their *pretense* of being interested in liberty. There are no guarantees for success, but to my way of thinking, it is far better to make one's stand and go down fighting for an ideal than to kneel quietly while our freedoms are being stripped away a little bit more each day.

Czechoslovakia, France, Great Britain, Rumania, Japan, Germany, Italy, South America, the United States—even tiny Switzerland—these nations and more have seen some form of turbulence over the past few years. The youth rebellion against governmental institutions is a worldwide phenomenon. In several nations—Czechoslovakia, France, Italy, sections of Latin America—the students have had the support of the middle class and consequently their efforts have been more disruptive. If the biggest victims of state interventionism—the great, productive American middle—could be aroused, the repercussions against statism and changes in favor of liberty would be felt around the world.

In the entire history of man on earth, the American experiment in open, multiracial democracy stands as a colossus among the ruins of past civilizations. Never before in history has so much creativity, so much energy, so much talent and productivity burst forth in one place and at one precise moment. Unfortunately, the grotesque horror of slavery marred our beginnings as a society which claimed to offer equal opportunity for every individual. Even the more libertarian of our forefathers compromised their theoretical principles through the exploitation of human life and labor. But the ideals expressed by men like Thomas Jefferson, and the revolutionary fire represented in the Declaration of Independence, will outlive the flawed translation of these ideals into actual practice.

The catalyst that made all this possible was the ideal of *liberty* and *freedom*, an approximation of a truly open society in which each individual should be free to act in accordance with his own rational self-determination as a self-owned entity.

Now all this is being destroyed. The American heritage, our birthright as a society of free individuals, is being trampled by an army of bureaucratic politicians who have been nurtured in the miasma of a philosophical swampland. Relativistic values have displaced absolutes; relativistic ethical codes have displaced moral conviction; pragmatism has displaced objective reasoning as the motive power for human activity.

All this must be stopped before we destroy ourselves and the remnant of liberty that remains to us today. It must be stopped finally and conclusively and be replaced by the burning fire of liberty that once blazed in the hearts of man.

America! Once you held a dream for all of man.

Now that dream must be fulfilled, or we shall all perish with its destruction.

THE REVOLUTION COMES TO YAF

ANARCHY FOREVER!

POWER TO THE PEOPLE . . . SOCK IT TO THE STATE!

I AM AN ENEMY OF THE STATE!

FUCK THE DRAFT!

LEAVE US ALONE . . . LAISSEZ FAIRE . . . LEAVE US ALONE!

NO MORE VIETNAMS!

STOP THE KILLING . . . END THE GENOCIDE!

POWER TO THE NEIGHBORHOODS!

POWER TO THE PEOPLE!

A New Left rally? An SDS convention? A Black Panther strategy conference? Not quite.

The *place* was Stouffer's Riverfront Inn, St. Louis, Missouri.

The *Time*, August 28–31, 1969.

The *occasion*, the bi-annual National Convention of the "conservative" student organization, Young Americans for Freedom.

It had been apparent for more than six months that the leadership of YAF, a traditionally conservative youth organization since its inception in 1960, was being challenged from within by a persistent group of disaffected intellectuals. Just how strong they were, how many they numbered, was impossible to say. Their presence within YAF was revealed now and then through publication in *The New Guard*, the official YAF magazine, of an occasional article dealing with anarchist philosophy or the organization and operation of an anarchist society. But, by and large, *The New Guard* reflected the conservative thinking of the majority of its readership.

The exact nature of the philosophical differences dividing the conservatives and anarcho-libertarians has been covered earlier in detail. Everybody knows who William F. Buckley is and what he stands for. Or Reagan. Or Goldwater. Briefly, what the anarchists and libertarians on the Right have been saying with increasing frequency is that, if the conservatives actually believed in their stated ideology of limited government and individual freedom, they would not be supporting U.S. genocide in Vietnam and they would not be trying to preserve and protect the immense power of state-corporate fascism which serves as the current form of government in this nation. They would instead be organizing anti-war groups and anti-draft committees; they would be defending individual liberty in the black community against the mindless oppression of the white policeman; they would be supporting many of the Supreme Court decisions of recent years which favor the rights of the individual against the authoritarianism of the state. They would in short be doing everything the New Left is now doing, for different reasons perhaps, with different emphasis on the various issues perhaps, but nevertheless they would be acting to reduce the power of the state in its dealings with the many individuals who constitute our society.

Instead, they have been doing the exact opposite; and this is the issue which the YAF dissidents brought into the open during the convention in St. Louis.

On the surface, there was no indication of any major confrontation arising at the convention. Key speakers for the occasion, secured by the conservative YAF leadership, included the usual right-wing luminaries: William F. Buckley, Frank Meyer, William Rusher, Al Capp (Yes, Al Capp!), Fulton Lewis III, Barry Goldwater, Jr., Phyllis Schlafly, and Phillip Abbott Luce. Major emphasis in the various seminars was placed on formulating an effective strategy for combating the New Left on campus. If one merely read the proposed agenda circulated several weeks before the convention, it promised to be a routine excoriation of everyone to the left

of Richard Nixon and Billy Graham, with maybe
a few wrist-slapping comments for George Wallace and the fire-breathing ultra-right.

However, several hours before the opening session
a group of New York rebels distributed the August
15th issue of *The Libertarian Forum* which contained an open letter to the convention from Dr.
Murray N. Rothbard. Rothbard has been interested
in forging a Left/Right coalition for several years,
and since the beginning of 1969 he and Karl Hess
have actively been recruiting libertarian New Leftists and dissident Rightists into their Radical Libertarian Alliance, an organization which openly endorses revolution (visible self-defense against the
violence of the government) as the most effective
means of achieving a free and open society.

In his letter, Dr. Rothbard spoke directly to those
libertarian YAFers who had been growing increasingly discontent with the policies of the YAF
leadership:

. . . this letter is a plea that you use the occasion of
the public forum of the YAF convention to go, to split,
to leave the conservative movement. . . .

What has YAF, in its *action programs*, ever done on
behalf of the free market? Its only action related to the
free market has been to *oppose* it, to call for embargoes
on Polish hams and other products from Eastern Europe. . . .

They [conservatives] hate the Warren Court almost
as much as they do Reds for "coddling criminals," and
the cry goes up everywhere for all power to the police.

What can be more profoundly statist, despotic, and anti-libertarian than that?

Why don't you get out, form your own organization, breathe the clean air of freedom, and then take your stand, proudly and squarely, not with the despotism of the power elite and the government of the United States, but with the rising movement in opposition to that government?

At the same time, rumors were circulated that Karl Hess was arriving in St. Louis to address the convention on opening night. Since he was not a scheduled speaker, the implication was that a demonstration would have to be staged by the radicals to demand that Hess be given a chance to express the opposition point of view. The conservatives, applying their overkill mentality to this potential crisis, were visibly dismayed by the fact that the rebels had come up with a "name" speaker of their own. That the YAF leadership had loaded the convention with some sixteen hardline conservatives of impeccable *anti-Communist* credentials was, apparently, not enough. The enemy had come up with Hess as a gesture of defiance and the only thing to do was "escalate" their side of the conflict.

To make matters worse for the conservative point of view, Barry Goldwater, Jr., sent word prior to the convention—evidently upon hearing that there might be some "trouble" in St. Louis—that he could not attend. He suddenly felt a need to be with his constituents over the Labor Day weekend.

At approximately 4:30 P.M., just three and a half

hours before William F. Buckley was scheduled to
deliver the opening address, Karl Hess' son, Karl
Hess IV, received word that his father would not be
permitted to speak on the floor of the convention.
Many of the anarchist and radical libertarian delegates also discovered that they were having diffi-
culty receiving the proper credentials which would
admit them for the voting session on Saturday.
Young Hess announced to the press that a 'mini-
convention' would be held under the Arch, the
symbolic gateway to the west, at 11 P.M., following
Buckley's speech. His father was arriving later that
evening and would speak to any dissident YAFers
who wished to hear his remarks.

Realizing that a major split was underway—made
all the more apparent by the heavy television and
press attention the anarchists were receiving as
they arrived in St. Louis with their black flags un-
furled—William F. Buckley called a press conference at 5:30 P.M. Buckley was questioned mainly
as to the nature and seriousness of the imminent
split which now threatened to disrupt the entire
convention. He denied that the confrontation was
serious, claiming that the dissident element was too
miniscule to be of any real importance. At this
point, Karl Hess IV, leader of YAF's Anarcho-libertarian Alliance, Walter Block, and myself, acting as
spokesmen for the Radical Libertarian Alliance,
broke into the conference and publicly invited
Buckley to debate with Hess under the Arch later
that night, since the YAF leadership would not provide for such an encounter as part of the official

proceedings. Buckley declined, stating that he had an article to write that evening and in any event he did not think the issue was important enough that it could not wait until a later date.

Now the breach was visible, having been made an issue in Buckley's own press conference, and the only question that now remained was *how many* dissident YAFers would split off to the open-air meeting in support of the opposition. The matter remained in abeyance until 8 P.M., at which time the convention was officially declared open. Before Mr. Buckley could be introduced to the crowd, a delegation of California anarchists staged a demonstration, demanding that their chapter chairman, Pat Dowd, who had earlier been dismissed for his radical views, be given a seat with the delegates on the stage. The demonstration would have remained a procedural one, rotating around the seating of the ousted chairman, had the conservatives not sent up a ringing chant in support of Buckley. Cries of, "We want Buckley! We want Buckley!" now dinned throughout the ballroom, only to be met with the opposition call, "We want Hess! We want Hess!"

It was only now that the press and the conventioners themselves had a chance to estimate the size of the dissident faction. The ferocity of the cries in opposition to the conservatives clearly startled the traditionalist contingent which now started chanting the official slogan of the convention:

"Sock it to the Left! Sock it to the Left!"

"Sock it to the State! Sock it to the State!" was the answer to this new attempt to drown them out.

Finally, after a half hour delay during which the ousted California chairman succeeded in claiming his seat upon the stage, William F. Buckley rose to deliver the official opening remarks of the convention.

The fact that he was more than just a little concerned over the size of the opposition forces present in the hall was immediately apparent by the direction of his speech. The first fifteen minutes was devoted to a ringing denunciation of Rothbard's open letter to the convention and criticism of some remarks made by Karl Hess in the same issue of their *Libertarian Forum.* As usual for Buckley, his excoriation dealt with the style rather than the content of the letter, as if the main crime committed was their bad manners in confronting the issues head on rather than fondling them like gentlemen. He continued his speech with the usual conservative tirade about the perils of international communism and our need to arm ourselves at all costs and defend our nation even "unto the consummation of the world."

Presumably we would all go to heaven with the Pope for blowing up the earth in the name of God.

Another interesting fact worth mentioning is Mr. Buckley's attitude on the question of freedom. In his speech he mentioned that freedom is for those who agree to live within the framework of our traditions. Those who deny these traditions become *excommunicants* who then lose their right to the freedom guaranteed by our constitutional republic. Here, precisely, is the mystical element in the conservative

mentality which has pushed conservatives so far
apart from their former allies: the notion that freedom is a gift to be dispensed among our worthy
citizens by a moralistic government. The anarchists
claim that freedom is a natural right, and if the
state denies it to its citizens, they have a right to seize
it themselves.

At 11 P.M., following the opening ceremonies, a
slow trickle of students began heading for the sil-
ver arch dazzling in the moonlight. Gradually their
numbers grew, swelling to a crowd of some three
hundred sprawled along the hillside beneath the arch
facing the Mississippi. Hess, surrounded by his son
and other leaders of the radical faction, then delivered his now familiar message. The Right had
abandoned its stated principles championing the individual. Power to the People was formerly an old
Republican concept and was now a policy of the
New Left. The conservatives, heretofore critical of
our expanding federal bureaucracy, were now ag-
grandizing more power to the state in order to fight
"the Communist menace." The chief threat to
liberty in the United States was *not* the splintered
radical Left, but the efficient and near-omnipotent
United States government. Decentralization and
neighborhood control was the only answer for the
growing urban crisis, and the Right must join forces
with the New Left in a united attempt to realize
these goals.

The Hess message was a popular one for those
assembled on the hillside—an estimated twenty to
twenty-five percent of the total 1200 attending the

convention—but his endorsement of a Libertarian Right and New Left coalition clearly polarized the group into two broad camps. The more radical element was enthusiastic about joining forces with at least some libertarian (voluntary commune) factions of the New Left; the more conservative were visibly disturbed and registered some doubts about the "inherent totalitarian tendencies" of collectivism, whether voluntary or otherwise. After Hess' speech, the crowd broke up into discussion groups, and that's how the night ended at approximately 3 A.M., with a dozen units of concerned students debating issues under the stars.

The main hope of the conservatives the following morning was to divide their opposition into two weak and ineffectual camps. These would be the more "conservative" libertarians who were interested in working within YAF to elect their own directors to the National Board which was completely controlled by hard-line Buckleyites and to adopt a few libertarian planks into the official platform, calling for: active resistance against the draft; a denunciation of domestic fascism as a twin evil to international communism; legalization of marijuana; immediate pull-out from Vietnam; several changes in YAF's official Sharon Statement; and an assortment of other pertinent resolutions. These libertarians, led by Don Ernsberger and Dana Rohrabacher, were by far the larger of the two dissident groups, claiming over three hundred members for their Libertarian Caucus.

The second faction of rebels consisted of radical

libertarians or anarchists, most of them belonging to Karl Hess IV's Anarcho-libertarian Alliance. This contingent was more interested in splitting off from YAF entirely and forming a new alliance with New Left anarchists and anti-statists. They numbered no more than fifty hard-core radicals but had high hopes of siphoning off as many of the libertarian group as possible by the end of the convention.

The second day proceeded fairly well along the lines that the conservatives had planned. There were addresses in the morning by Stephen Shadegg, a Goldwater biographer, and Dr. Harold Demsetz of the University of Chicago. The afternoon offered a panel consisting of Frank Meyer, William Rusher, and Phillip Crane, who discussed the Communist threat in America. The most horrifying segment of the day came during the evening session when Fulton Lewis III and Representative "Buz" Lukens delivered two blistering speeches, explicitly calling for strong federal powers in order to combat the expanding menace of international communism. Except for Dr. Demsetz's speech in the morning enumerating various benefits of the free market, the general tone of the day was fundamentally conservative, hammering away at the negative theme of anti-communism.

If Friday was a field day for the conservatives, Saturday would be remembered as the day on which all those of even quasi-libertarian sentiment consolidated their forces in general disgust against the whole tone of the convention. The session opened at 11:30 A.M., an hour and a half later than sched-

uled. The first ninety minutes were occupied by
challenges from the floor on the seating of delegates,
with the libertarians charging that many of their
people were being purged by the conservative leadership in order to minimize their strength during the
voting for directors to the National Board and on
platform resolutions.

Finally the roll call of states began. The Libertarian Caucus was basing its hope on a slate of nine
candidates ranging ideologically from moderate
libertarian to anarchist. If two or three of their
candidates were elected, and perhaps one or two
of their minority plank resolutions passed, the Erns-
berger group would have considered it a victory
and divorced themselves entirely from the radical
Anarcho-libertarian Alliance. However, this was
not to be the case. Before half the role was called,
it was evident that every one of the libertarian candidates was being thoroughly routed and the conservatives eventually succeeded in electing all their
candidates to the nine available positions. At this
point talk of a walk-out began to spread for the
first time into the ranks of the moderate libertarians.

Next came the voting on the minority platform
resolutions. Disaffection spread rapidly among the
entire opposition as, one by one, they saw their resolutions hammered down by the conservatives: immediate withdrawal from Vietnam—defeated; legalization of marijuana—tabled; denunciation of domestic
fascism—hooted down and defeated. Then came the
issue which finally polarized the convention into
two hostile, openly-warring camps. The libertarians

offered their resolution advocating active resistance to the military draft and saw it trammeled by a solid majority. After the reading of the majority plank on the draft which limited anti-draft agitation to legal channels, the event took place which was to force everyone present to make an instant decision: to support the conservative majority, or oppose them along with the radical libertarians. There could no longer be any room for fence-straddling.

A young man, who shall remain nameless for obvious reasons, stepped forward and grabbed a microphone in the center of the floor. Clearly announcing that it was the right of every individual to defend himself from violence, including state violence, he raised a card, touched it with a flame from a cigarette lighter, and lifted it over his head while it burned freely into a curling black ash. For fifteen or twenty seconds the hall was locked in numb silence, finally to be shattered by an enraged war cry:

"Kill the commies!"

The next second can be best described as the instant radicalization of the moderate libertarians. While the first onrushers were knocked back by five or six radicals surrounding the "criminal commie," the ranks of the Libertarian Caucus solidified into a barrier separating the radicals from the howling conservative majority. In the swinging and pushing which followed, the young student who had triggered the melee escaped outside the convention hall. The libertarians, stepping onto chairs and raising their fists against the conservatives, sent up a chant:

"Laissez faire! Laissez faire!"

There was no question where they stood now: in clear opposition to the conservative majority.

The majority found their own voices and howled back in reply:

"We want Barry! We want Barry!"

This was met with cries of:

"We want freedom! We want freedom!"

Then:

"Sock it to the Left! Sock it to the Left!"
was countered with:

"Sock it to the State! Sock it to the State!"

The issues were clearly drawn, and three hundred and fifty libertarians suddenly found themselves in violent opposition to their former conservative allies numbering some eight or nine hundred strong. It took the best part of the next half hour to calm everyone down and get them outside the convention hall. In the following early evening hours, the conservatives met privately and passed a resolution condemning the card-burning act as "illegal," and denouncing the radicals as being "outside the mainstream of Young Americans for Freedom" (echoes of 1964).

This was not the end of the visible conflict separating the two groups. Later that night, while the libertarians were conducting their own meeting to discuss future strategy, a swarm of conservatives went stomping through the floors of the inn shouting: "Kill the libertarians! Kill the libertarians!" Suddenly it dawned on the minority opposition exactly who their main enemy really was. The New Left? New Leftists had never demanded the blood

of the anti-statist Right. The situation was so shock-
ing to some of the instantly-radicalized that there
was even talk of traveling only in groups and lock-
ing themselves into their rooms.

However, this defensive attitude did not last for
any length of time. The smell of success had been
too exhilarating. In the corridor outside the main
convention hall, Dana Rohrabacher, Don Erns-
berger, and several of the "moderate" libertarian
group were actually setting the pace for the radical
anarchists. The former moderates were now paint-
ing placards with anarchist slogans—'Smash the
State!" "Fuck the Draft!" "I am an enemy of the
State!"—and posting them up on the walls. While a
chorus of boos greeted them from conservative on-
lookers, Rohrabacher mounted a chair and started
the now-familiar cry:

"Laissez faire! Laissez faire!"

This was picked up instantly by about one hundred fifty of the former moderates, and now it was
their turn to go tromping through the corridors
of the hotel, forcing the conservatives to scurry
into locked rooms. When the counter-demonstra-
tion finally exhausted itself, the conservatives managed to muster a small counter-counter-offensive,
chanting the cry, "Lazy fairies!" as they passed the
radicals, thereby putting themselves in the unique
position of repudiating their own economic philosophy and openly embracing our current system
of state-corporate fascism.

The climax of the convention for the radicals
came in the form of a meeting held later in the night.

During the meeting, attended by people from Erns-berger's Libertarian Caucus, young Karl Hess' An-archo-libertarian Alliance, the New York-based Radical Libertarian Alliance, Skye D'Aureous' Lib-ertarian Connection, two SDS anarchist chapters, and several other radical groups, a communications network was established to keep all the organiza-tions, including any New Left organizations that care to participate, in continuous contact with one another. This new loosely-knit organization is now called the Society for Individual Liberty and will be managed and operated from its headquarters in Maryland.

Some of the radicals have split off entirely from YAF; others will remain on an individual basis and continue to proselytize among the conservative ranks. The most important thing to emerge from this convention is that, for the first time, the most influential forces on the Libertarian Right will be working to establish an open and working coalition with the New Left in their common struggle to resist the abuses of the United States government.